101 CAKES & COOKIES
TRIED-AND-TESTED RECIPES

Hylas Publishing
Publisher: Sean Moore
Creative Director: Karen Prince
Designer: Gus Yoo
Editor: Sarah Postle

First published in by BBC Worldwide Ltd,
Woodlands,

80 Wood Lane, London W12 OTT All photographs
© *BBC Good Food Magazine* 2004

All the recipes contained in this book first appeared
in *BBC Good Food Magazine*.

Published in the United States by
Hylas Publishing
129 Main Street, Irvington,
New York 10533

Copyright © BBC Worldwide 2004

The moral right of the author has been asserted.

Commissioning Editor: Vivien Bowler
Project Editor: Warren Albers
Designers: Kathryn Gammon and Annette Peppis
Design Manager: Sarah Ponder
Production Controller: Arlene Alexander

First American Edition published in 2003
02 03 04 05 10 9 8 7 6 5 4 3 2 1

ISBN 1-59258-104-8

Set in Bookman Old Style, Helvetica and ITC
Officina Sans

Printed and bound in Italy by LEGO SpA

Color origination by Radstock Reproductions Ltd.

Distributed by National Book Network

101 CAKES & COOKIES
TRIED-AND-TESTED RECIPES

Editor-in-chief
Mary Cadogan

HYLAS
PUBLISHING

Contents

Introduction

When the stresses of everyday life start to get to me, I find a session in the kitchen doing a bit of light cake making is the perfect answer. Cake making is sheer indulgence – nobody really needs a cake – though that's part of the pleasure. And the simple actions of beating together butter and sugar, folding in flour and rubbing mixtures together are enormously therapeutic.

Add to that the delicious smells that fill the house and the delight of all who share your baked offering, and the pleasure is complete. And whatever you make, it will always be a million times better than anything you could buy.

The cakes, biscuits and bakes in this book are all essentially very simple to make whether you are a beginner or an experienced baker, and you won't need loads of special equipment. You will find every cake you would ever want to make in these pages, from the classic recipes for shortbread and flapjacks, to exciting new ideas such as *Blueberry Cheesecake Gateau*, *Pumpkin and Ginger Teabread* and *Strawberry and Cinnamon Torte*.

So why wait? Get out your mixing bowl and spoon and get baking – you know it makes sense.

Mary Cadoga

Mary Cadogan
Food Director
BBC Good Food Magazine

Conversion tables

NOTES ON THE RECIPES
• Eggs are large, unless stated otherwise.
• Wash all fresh produce before preparation.

OVEN TEMPERATURES

°F	°C	Gas	Fan °C	Oven temp.
225	110	¼	90	Very cool
250	120	½	100	Very cool
275	140	1	120	Cool or slow
300	150	2	130	Cool or slow
325	160	3	140	Warm
350	180	4	160	Moderate
375	190	5	170	Moderately hot
400	200	6	180	Fairly hot
425	220	7	200	Hot
450	230	8	210	Very hot
475	240	9	220	Very hot

APPROXIMATE WEIGHT CONVERSIONS
• All the recipes in this book use American measurements. The charts on this page and the next will help you convert to metric measurements. Conversions are approximate and have been rounded up or down. Follow one set of measurements only; do not mix the two.
• Cup measurements have not been listed here, because they vary from ingredient to ingredient. Please use kitchen scales to weigh dry/solid ingredients.

SPOON MEASURES

- Spoon measurements are level unless otherwise specified.
- 1 teaspoon = 5ml
- 1 tablespoon = 15ml
- 1 Australian tablespoon = 20ml (cooks in Australia should measure 3 teaspoons where 1 tablespoon is specified in a recipe)

APPROXIMATE LIQUID CONVERSIONS

US	Metric	Imperial	Australia
¼ cup	50ml	2fl oz	¼ cup
½ cup	125ml	4fl oz	½ cup
¾ cup	175ml	6fl oz	¾ cup
1 cup	225ml	8fl oz	1 cup
1¼ cups	300ml	10fl oz/½ pint	½ pint
2 cups/1 pint	450ml	16fl oz	2 cups
2½ cups	600ml	20fl oz/1 pint	1 pint
1 quart	1 litre	35fl oz/1¾ pints	1¾ pints

A special-occasion cake from *Good Food* reader
and baker Carrie Hill.

Cherry and Marzipan Cake

8oz butter, softened
8oz caster sugar
4 eggs, beaten
8oz self-raising flour
8oz glacé cherries, chopped
4oz ground almonds
2–3 drops almond extract
9oz marzipan
2oz blanched almonds,
halved lengthways
icing sugar, for dusting

Takes 1 hour 55 minutes • Serves 12

1 Preheat oven to 325°F. Butter and line a deep 8in round cake pan. Beat the butter and sugar in a bowl until light and creamy. Pour in the eggs a little at a time and beat well after each addition. Mix in the flour one third at a time.

2 Fold in the cherries, ground almonds and almond extract until evenly mixed. Spoon half the mixture into the pan.

3 Roll out the marzipan to a 7½in circle. Lay this on top of the cake mixture in the pan, then cover with the rest of the mixture. Level, and sprinkle the almonds on top.

4 Bake for 1½ hours, or until a skewer inserted comes out clean, covering with foil after 1 hour. Leave to cool in the tin for 20 minutes, then turn out on to a wire rack and cool completely. Dust with icing sugar.

• Per serving 479 calories, protein 8g, carbohydrate 57g, fat 26g, saturated fat 10g, fiber 2g, added sugar 35g, salt 0.57g

This cake is based on a recipe by food writer Geraldene Holt, who lived in Devon, England for many years.

Devonshire Honey Cake

8oz unsalted butter
9oz clear honey, plus about
2 tbsp extra to glaze
4oz dark muscovado sugar
3 large eggs, beaten
10oz self-raising flour

Takes 1½ hours • Serves 12

1 Preheat oven to 325°F. Butter and line a 8in round loose-bottomed cake tin. Cut the butter into pieces and drop into a medium pan with the honey and sugar. Melt slowly over a low heat. When liquid, increase the heat under the pan and boil for about one minute. Leave to cool.

2 Beat the eggs into the cooled honey mixture using a wooden spoon. Sift the flour into a large bowl and pour in the egg and honey mixture, beating until you have a smooth batter.

3 Pour the mixture into the pan and bake for 50 minutes–1 hour until the cake is well-risen, golden brown and springs back when pressed.

4 Turn the cake out on a wire rack. Warm 2 tablespoons of honey in a small pan and brush over the top of the cake to glaze, then leave to cool.

• Per serving 336 calories, protein 4g, carbohydrate 43g, fat 17g, saturated fat 10g, fiber 1g, added sugar 25g, salt 0.29g

Dump it all into a bowl, give it a quick beat
and it's ready to bake.

Cinnamon Nutella Cake

6oz butter, softened
6oz golden caster sugar
3 eggs
8oz self-raising flour
1 tsp baking powder
2 tsp ground cinnamon
4 tbsp milk
4 rounded tbsp chocolate hazelnut spread
2oz hazelnuts, roughly chopped

Takes 1½ hours • Serves 12

1 Preheat oven to 350°F. Butter and line the base of an 8in round cake pan.
2 Put the butter, sugar, eggs, flour, baking powder, cinnamon and milk into a bowl. Beat until light and fluffy.
3 Pour three quarters of the mixture into the tin, spread it level, then spoon the hazelnut spread on in four blobs. Top with the remaining mixture, swirl a few times with a skewer, then smooth.
4 Sprinkle with the nuts. Bake for 1 hour–1 hour 10 minutes, until risen, nicely browned, feels firm to the touch and springs back when lightly pressed (cover with foil if it starts to brown too quickly). Cool in the pan for 10 minutes, then turn out, peel off the paper and cool on a wire rack.

• Per serving 320 calories, protein 5g, carbohydrate 34g, fat 19g, saturated fat 8g, fiber 1g, added sugar 20g, salt 0.63g

Remind yourself of the lovely moist flavor of coconut
with this nostalgic bake.

Coconut Cake

6oz butter, softened
6oz golden caster sugar
6oz self-raising flour
1½ tsp baking powder
3 eggs, beaten
2oz desiccated coconut
2 tbsp coconut cream, or single
cream

FOR THE BUTTERCREAM
FILLING AND TOPPING
10oz icing sugar
4oz butter, softened
3 tbsp coconut cream, or single
cream
5 tbsp raspberry jam

Takes 45 minutes • Serves 8

1 Preheat oven to 350°F. Butter two 8in sandwich tins and line the bases with greaseproof paper. Mix the butter, sugar, flour, baking powder and eggs in a food processor for 2–3 minutes until smooth. Gently stir in the coconut and cream.

2 Divide the mixture between the pans and smooth the tops. Bake for 25 minutes until evenly golden and firm. Loosen the edges and leave in the pans for 5 minutes, then turn out on to a wire rack to cool. Peel off the lining paper.

3 Make the buttercream: beat together the icing sugar, butter and coconut cream until smooth. Spread one sponge with the jam. Top with just under half the buttercream and sandwich with the other sponge. Swirl the remaining buttercream on top of the cake.

• Per serving 410 calories, protein 9g, carbohydrate 42g, fat 23g, saturated fat 13g, fiber 1g, added sugar 14g, salt 1.22g

This egg-free cake is a real treat – it's packed with fruit and cinnamon.

Carrot, Apple and Raisin Cake

8oz self-raising flour
½ tsp baking powder
½ tsp salt
1 tsp ground cinnamon
5 tbsp vegetable oil
grated zest of 1 orange plus
4 tbsp juice
5oz light muscovado sugar
5oz finely grated carrot
1 medium eating apple, peeled,
cored and grated
3oz raisins
2oz pumpkin seeds
icing sugar, for dusting

Takes 1 hour 40 minutes • Serves 12

1 Preheat oven to 350°F. Butter an 8in round cake pan. Mix the flour, baking powder, salt and cinnamon together in a large bowl. In a separate bowl mix together the oil, orange juice and sugar.

2 Add the orange mixture to the flour along with the grated carrot and apple, orange zest, raisins and pumpkin seeds and stir until really well mixed. Spoon into the prepared pan.

3 Bake for 50 minutes–1 hour, until the cake pulls from the side of the pan. Cool on a rack before removing from tin. Dust with icing sugar and serve.

• Per serving 207 calories, protein 3g, carbohydrate 36g, fat 7g, saturated fat 1g, fiber 1g, added sugar 13g, salt 0.47g

This traditional cake will keep for up to two weeks.

Authentic Yorkshire Parkin

1 egg
3 tbsp milk
6oz golden syrup
4oz molasses
3oz light muscovado sugar
8oz butter
4oz medium oatmeal
9oz plain flour
2 rounded tsp ground ginger
2 tsp baking soda

Takes 1 hour 10 minutes • Serves 16

1 Preheat oven to 325°F. Butter a deep 9in square cake pan and line. Beat the egg and stir in the milk, then set aside.

2 Put the syrup, molasses, sugar and butter in a large pan and heat gently until the sugar has dissolved and the butter has melted. Remove from the heat. Mix together the oatmeal, flour, ginger and baking soda, then stir into the syrup mixture, followed by the egg and milk. Combine well.

3 Pour the mixture into the pan and bake for 50 minutes–1 hour until the cake feels firm and a little crusty on top. Leave to cool in the pan, then turn out and peel off the paper. Wrap the parkin in clean greaseproof paper and foil and leave it for at least three days – this allows it to become much softer and stickier.

• Per serving 261 calories, protein 3g, carbohydrate 36g, fat 13g, saturated fat 8g, fiber 1g, added sugar 18g, salt 0.38g

You can store this cake for up to a week in a cake dome.

Raisin Spice Cake

FOR THE TOPPING
1oz butter
1oz demerara sugar
1 tsp mixed spice
1oz chopped nuts

FOR THE CAKE
3/4cup unsweetened orange juice
6oz raisins
6oz butter
6oz light muscovado sugar
9oz self-raising flour
1 tsp mixed spice
1 tsp ground cinnamon
1 tsp ground ginger
3 eggs, beaten

Takes 1 hour 20 minutes •
Serves 10–12

1 Preheat oven to 325°F. Butter a 9in ring tin or 8in round cake pan. Make the topping: chop the butter into the topping ingredients, then sprinkle in the pan.
2 Pour the juice into a pan, then add the raisins, butter and sugar. Bring to a boil, stirring, then simmer for 5 minutes.
3 Lift off the heat; cool for 10 minutes. Sift the flour, mixed spice, cinnamon and ginger into the pan, then add the eggs and mix. Pour into the pan and smooth the top.
4 Bake for 45 minutes until firm. Cool in the pan for 5 minutes, then transfer on to a wire rack to cool completely.

• Per serving (for ten) 408 calories, protein 6g, carbohydrate 54g, fat 20g, saturated fat 11g, fiber 1g, added sugar 20g, salt 0.75g

A lovely moist cake that gets even better if left undisturbed
in the cake pan for a couple of days.

Porter Cake

6oz butter
1lb mixed dried fruit
grated zest and juice of 1 orange
6oz light muscovado sugar
7fl oz porter, Guinness or
Caffrey's
1 tsp baking soda
3 eggs, beaten
10oz plain flour
2 tsp mixed spice

FOR THE TOPPING
2 tbsp flaked almonds
2 tbsp demerara sugar

Takes 2 hours 25 minutes • Serves 12

1 Preheat oven to 300°F. Butter and line the base of a deep 8in round cake pan. Put the butter, dried fruit, orange zest and juice, sugar and porter in a large pan. Bring slowly to a boil, stirring until the butter has dissolved, then simmer for 15 minutes.
2 Cool for 10 minutes, then stir in the baking soda. The mixture will foam up, but don't worry, this is normal.
3 Stir the eggs into the pan, then sift in the flour and spice and mix well. Pour into the prepared tin, smooth the top with the back of a spoon and sprinkle with the flaked almonds and demerara sugar. Bake for 1¼–1½ hours. Cool in the pan for 15 minutes, then turn out and cool on a wire rack.

• Per serving 400 calories, protein 6g, carbohydrate 63g, fat 15g, saturated fat 8g, fiber 2g, added sugar 17g, salt 0.69g

You can make the cake a couple of days in advance,
wrap well, then ice on the day of serving.

Sticky Ginger Cake
with Ginger Fudge Icing

8oz unsalted butter, diced
6oz molasses sugar
3 tbsp molasses
½ cup milk
2 large eggs, beaten
4 pieces stem ginger, drained from
their syrup, chopped
10oz self-raising flour
1 tbsp ground ginger

FOR THE ICING
4 tbsp ginger syrup, drained from jar
10oz golden icing sugar, sifted
5oz unsalted butter, softened
2 tsp lemon juice

Takes 1 hour 10 minutes • Serves 16

1 Preheat oven to 325°F. Butter and line the base of a 9in round cake pan. Gently melt the butter, sugar and **molasses**; cool briefly, then stir in the milk. Beat in the eggs and add the chopped stem ginger. Sift the flour, ground ginger and a pinch of salt into the warm mixture. Combine thoroughly.

2 Spoon the cake mixture into the pan and level the surface. Bake for 30–35 minutes or until firm and risen. Cool in the pan for an hour, then transfer to a wire rack.

3 Skewer the top of the cooled cake all over, then pour 2 tablespoons of the syrup over. Beat together the icing sugar, butter, lemon juice and the remaining ginger syrup, and spread over the cake.

• Per serving 379 calories, protein 3g, carbohydrate 53g, fat 19g, saturated fat 11g, fiber 1g, added sugar 37g, salt 0.27g

Light and enticingly moist, this cake keeps
for up to a week in a tin.

Yummy Scrummy Carrot Cake

6oz light muscovado sugar
6fl oz sunflower oil
3 large eggs, lightly beaten
5oz grated carrot (about
3 medium carrots)
4oz raisins
grated zest of 1 large orange
6oz self-raising flour
1 tsp bicarbonate of soda
1 tsp ground cinnamon
½ tsp grated nutmeg (freshly grated
will give you the best flavor)

FOR THE FROSTING
6oz icing sugar
1½–2 tbsp orange juice

Takes 1¼ hours • Serves 15

1 Preheat oven to 350°F. Oil and line the base and sides of a 7in square cake tin. Tip the sugar into a large mixing bowl, pour in the oil and add the eggs. Lightly mix, then stir in the grated carrots, raisins and orange rind.
2 Mix the flour, soda and spices, then sift into the bowl. Lightly mix all the ingredients.
3 Pour the mixture into the prepared tin and bake for 40–45 minutes, until it feels firm and springy when you press it in the center. Cool in the tin for 5 minutes, then turn it out, peel off the paper and cool on a wire rack.
4 Beat together the frosting ingredients in a small bowl until smooth. Set the cake on a serving plate and drizzle the icing over the top. Leave to set, then cut into slices.

• Per serving 265 calories, protein 3g, carbohydrate 39g, fat 12g, saturated fat 2g, fiber 1g, added sugar 24g, salt 0.41g

The flavor of the olive oil comes through along with the citrus fruits and the almonds.

Olive Oil Cake

1 orange
1 lemon
4 large eggs
4oz caster sugar
6oz plain flour
1 tbsp baking powder
8fl oz extra virgin olive oil
4oz blanched almonds,
toasted and finely chopped
icing sugar, for dusting

Takes 1 hour 25 minutes • Serves 12

1 Preheat oven to 350°F. Oil and line the base of a 9in loose-bottomed or springform round cake pan. Put the orange and lemon in a pan and cover with water. Bring to a boil and leave to simmer for 30 minutes until very soft. Drain and cool. Cut away the skin from the white pith and blend the skin to a puréed paste in a food processor.

2 In a large bowl, beat the eggs with the sugar for 7–8 minutes. Sift the flour, baking powder and a pinch of salt together, then fold lightly into the egg mixture along with the olive oil. Very gently fold in the almonds and puréed fruit skin, but don't overmix.

3 Pour the batter into the pan and bake for 45 minutes. Cool on a wire rack, then dust with icing sugar.

• Per serving 333 calories, protein 6g, carbohydrate 25g, fat 24g, saturated fat 3g, fiber 1g, added sugar 11g, salt 0.45g

Stays soft and moist in the middle, and the icing
sets to a crisp meringue-like coating.

Pecan Ginger Cake

8oz self-raising flour
4 tsp ground ginger
1 tsp baking powder
½ tsp salt
8oz butter
12oz golden syrup
4oz light muscovado sugar
4 eggs, beaten
4oz pecans, roughly chopped
4oz crystallized ginger,
chopped

FOR THE TOPPING AND DECORATION
6oz golden granulated sugar
1 egg white
pinch of cream of tartar
3oz sugar
4oz pecan halves

Takes 1 hour • Serves 10

1 Preheat oven to 350°F. Butter and line the base of two 8in cake pans. Sift together the flour, ginger, baking powder and salt. Rub in the butter until it resembles crumbs.
2 Beat in the syrup, sugar, eggs, pecans and ginger. Pour into the pans and bake for 45 minutes until firm. Cool in the pans for 10 minutes, then turn out on to a wire rack.
3 Put the golden sugar, egg white, cream of tartar and 2 tablespoons hot water in a bowl set over (not in) a pan of simmering water. Beat for 10 minutes. Layer the cakes with a little icing; swirl the rest over the top and sides.
4 Heat the sugar with four tablespoons of water until dissolved, then boil until caramel forms. Stir in the pecan halves, cool on an oiled baking sheet, then use to decorate.

• Per serving 659 calories, protein 7g, carbohydrate 90g, fat 33g, saturated fat 11g, fiber 2g, added sugar 43g, salt 1.3g

It's big, it's rich, it's moist – and impossible to resist.

Mocha Fudge Cake with Coffee Icing

FOR THE ICING
6oz plain chocolate, melted
2oz unsalted butter, melted
½ cup double-strength espresso
1 tsp vanilla extract
10oz icing sugar

FOR THE CAKE
10oz plain flour, plus extra
2 tsp baking powder
1 tsp vanilla extract
3 eggs, separated
4fl oz milk
4 tbsp instant coffee granules
3oz unsalted butter
10oz caster sugar
3oz plain chocolate, melted
4fl oz sour cream

Takes 1 hour 5 minutes, plus 4 hours chilling • Serves 10

1 Whisk together the cooled icing ingredients. Cover and chill for 3–4 hours.
2 Preheat oven to 350°F. Butter and flour two 8in cake pans. Sift the flour and baking powder. Stir the vanilla into the egg yolks. Heat half the milk to boiling point, stir in the coffee to dissolve, then add the rest of the milk and cool.
3 Cream the butter and 8oz of the caster sugar. Slowly whisk in the egg yolk mixture, then the melted chocolate. Fold in the sifted dry ingredients, the cooled milk and the sour cream. Whisk the egg whites until stiff; whisk in the remaining sugar to form firm peaks. Fold the egg whites into the cake mixture and pour into the pans. Bake for 30 minutes until risen. Cool, split each cake in two, and layer with the icing.

• Per serving 627 calories, protein 8g, carbohydrate 103g, fat 23g, saturated fat 13g, fiber 2g, added sugar 77g, salt 0.42g

This tall cake is spectacular, easy to make and
keeps for up to one day in the fridge.

Blueberry Cheesecake Gateau

9oz self-raising flour
1 tsp baking powder
8oz caster sugar
8oz butter, softened
4 large eggs
2 tsp vanilla extract
1 tbsp milk

FOR THE ICING AND DECORATION
14oz medium-fat cream cheese
grated zest of 2 limes and the
juice of 1
4oz icing sugar
8oz blueberries

Takes 1¼ hours, plus 30 minutes
decorating • Serves 12

1 Preheat oven to 350°F. Butter and line the
base of a deep 7in round cake pan.
2 Put the flour, baking powder, sugar, butter,
eggs and vanilla into a large bowl and beat
with an electric mixer on low speed until
everything is mixed together. Increase the
speed and whisk for 2 minutes. Stir in the milk.
3 Spoon the mixture into the pan and level
the top. Bake the cake for about 50–60
minutes, until the cake springs back when
lightly pressed, cool, then split into three
layers.
4 Beat the cream cheese until soft, then
beat in the lime zest and juice and the icing
sugar. Sandwich the cake back together with
two thirds of the cheese mixture, and spread
the rest on the top. Arrange the blueberries in
tight circles around the top of the cake.

• Per serving 380 calories, protein 8g, carbohydrate
43g, fat 21g, saturated fat 9g, fiber 1g, added sugar
27g, salt 0.69g

Make this cake the day before a picnic – it's sturdy and travels well.

Fresh Cherry Cake with a Hint of Cinnamon

5oz self-raising flour
½ tsp ground cinnamon
2oz golden caster sugar
1 egg
4 tbsp milk
3oz butter, melted
12oz juicy, ripe cherries, stalks and stones removed
icing sugar, for dusting

FOR THE TOPPING
1oz plain flour
¼ tsp ground cinnamon
1oz golden caster sugar
1oz butter, diced and softened

Takes 1 hour 5 minutes • Serves 8

1 Preheat oven to 350°F. Butter and line the base of a 8in round cake tin. Sift the flour, cinnamon and sugar into a bowl. Make a well and add the egg, milk and melted butter. Combine and beat to make a thick, smooth mixture. Spoon into the tin and smooth. Scatter the cherries over the mixture and gently press them in.

2 Tip all the topping ingredients into a bowl. Rub in the butter to make a crumb-like mixture, then work until it comes together in pea-sized pieces. Scatter this over the cherries.

3 Bake for 30–35 minutes until a skewer pushed into the center comes out clean. Leave in the tin until cool enough to handle, then tip on to a wire rack until completely cold.

• Per serving 247 calories, protein 3g, carbohydrate 32g, fat 12g, saturated fat 7g, fiber 1g, added sugar 12g, salt 0.46g

This is good warm, as a pudding with whipped cream,
or cold, as a moist fruity cake.

Rhubarb and Orange Cake

12oz prepared rhubarb, cut
into 1½in lengths
8oz golden caster sugar
finely grated zest and juice of
½ small orange
5oz butter, softened
2 eggs, beaten
½ tsp baking powder
3oz self-raising flour
4oz ground almonds

FOR THE TOPPING
1oz butter, melted
1oz light muscovado sugar
finely grated zest of ½ small orange
2oz slivered almonds
icing sugar, for dusting

Takes 1 hour 25 minutes, plus 1 hour
standing • Serves 6–8

1 Mix the rhubarb with 2oz of the caster
sugar and the orange zest. Set aside for
1 hour, stirring once or twice.
2 Preheat oven to 375°F. Butter and line the
base of a deep 9in round cake tin. Cream
the butter and remaining caster sugar. Add
the eggs, baking powder, flour and ground
almonds. Beat gently, but do not overmix.
Stir in the orange juice, spoon into the tin,
and level. Drain the rhubarb and spoon over
the mixture. Bake for 25 minutes. Meanwhile,
combine the butter, sugar, zest and almonds.
3 Reduce the oven to 350°F. Sprinkle the
topping over the cake and return to the oven
for 15–20 minutes or until firm. Cool in the tin,
then transfer to a rack. Dust with icing sugar.

• Per serving (for six) 548 calories, protein 9g,
carbohydrate 44g, fat 39g, saturated fat 16g, fiber 3g,
added sugar 41g, salt 0.74g

This cake conjures up the taste of the Caribbean.

St. Lucia Banana Cake

12oz self-raising flour
1 tsp bicarbonate of soda
2 tsp mixed spice
6oz light muscovado sugar
4 eggs
7fl oz sunflower oil
2 bananas, mashed
4oz pineapple, very finely chopped
finely grated rind and juice of 1 orange
4oz pack walnuts, roughly chopped

FOR THE FROSTING
2 x 7oz packs medium-fat cream cheese, at room temperature
8oz icing sugar
2oz honey-coated banana chips

Takes 1 hour 5 minutes • Serves 12

1 Preheat oven to 350°F. Butter and line two 8in sandwich tins. Sift the flour into a large bowl with the soda, mixed spice and sugar.
2 Whisk the eggs and the oil until smooth. Stir the egg mixture into the flour with the bananas, pineapple, orange rind and juice and walnuts; stir well. Divide between the prepared tins. Bake for 45 minutes until risen and firm. Cool for 10 minutes, then remove from the tins, peel off the paper and leave to cool completely.
3 Beat the cream cheese until smooth. Gradually add the icing sugar to give a smooth frosting. Spread half the frosting over one cake. Put the other cake on top. Spread over the remaining icing, swirling it with a palette knife. Sprinkle over the banana chips.

• Per serving 545 calories, protein 10g, carbohydrate 64g, fat 30g, saturated fat 3g, fiber 2g, added sugar 32g, salt 0.66g

A bold, unusual dessert that marries fruit and herbs.

Lemon Polenta Cake with Rosemary Syrup

6oz polenta
2oz plain flour
1½ tsp baking powder
¼ tsp salt
5 tbsp natural yogurt
5 tbsp groundnut oil, plus extra for greasing
grated rind of 2 lemons, plus 2 tbsp fresh lemon juice
2 eggs, plus 2 egg whites
14oz caster sugar
2 sprigs fresh rosemary, plus extra sprigs to decorate
fresh raspberries and Greek yogurt, to serve

Takes 1 hour 5 minutes • Serves 8–10

1 Preheat oven to 350°F. Sift the polenta, flour, baking powder and salt into a bowl. Tip the yogurt, oil, lemon rind and juice into a jug; stir to combine.

2 Beat the eggs and egg whites with half the sugar until creamy. Beat in the yogurt mixture until smooth, then fold in the dry ingredients. Pour the batter into a 2 pint lightly oiled, lined loaf tin. Bake for 40–45 minutes or until a skewer inserted comes out clean.

3 Put the remaining sugar in a pan with 7fl oz of water and the rosemary sprigs. Bring to a boil, then simmer for 10 minutes. Cool completely, then strain.

4 Cool the cake on a wire rack for 15 minutes. Prick the top and drizzle over half the rosemary syrup. Serve with the rosemary sprigs, raspberries, yogurt and extra syrup.

• Per serving (for eight) 390 calories, protein 6g, carbohydrate 74g, fat 10g, saturated fat 2g, fiber 1g, added sugar 53g, salt 0.43g

This crumbly cake is a terrific way to enjoy fresh cherries.

Fresh Cherry Almond Cake

5oz whole blanched almonds
9oz self-raising flour
5oz butter, cut into small pieces and softened
5oz caster sugar
2 eggs, beaten
4fl oz milk
10oz fresh cherries, stoned and patted dry
1oz flaked almonds

Takes 1½ hours • Serves 8

1 Preheat oven to 350°F. Butter and line the base of a 8in round, deep cake tin. Put the blanched almonds in a small pan and heat gently, shaking occasionally, until golden brown (about 10 minutes). Cool, then whiz in a food processor until finely ground.
2 Tip the flour into a bowl and stir in the ground almonds. Rub in the butter until the mixture is crumbly. Stir in the sugar, then add the eggs, milk and cherries; mix until combined, but don't overmix.
3 Spoon into the prepared tin and smooth the top, then sprinkle the flaked almonds on top. Bake for 1 hour 10 minutes until the cake is golden on top and firm to the touch. Cool in the tin for 10 minutes, then turn out on to a wire rack to cool. Eat within 3 days.

• Per serving 474 calories, protein 10g, carbohydrate 48g, fat 28g, saturated fat 11g, fiber 2.8g, added sugar 18g, salt 0.69g

Serve this warm from the oven as a tasty dessert,
or cold for a picnic or lunchbox treat.

Apple and Cinnamon Cake

9oz self-raising flour
1 tsp ground cinnamon
1 tsp baking powder
4oz light muscovado sugar
6oz sultanas or raisins
4fl oz sunflower oil
2 eggs, beaten
4fl oz apple juice
2 dessert apples (not peeled), grated
1oz slivered or flaked almonds
icing sugar, for dusting

Takes 1 hour • Serves 8–10

1 Preheat oven to 350°F. Line a 9in round deep cake tin with baking paper. Sift the flour into a bowl with the cinnamon and baking powder, then stir in the sugar and sultanas. Make a well in the center and stir in the oil, eggs, apple juice and grated apple until well mixed.

2 Pour the mixture into the tin, scatter with almonds, then bake for 40–45 minutes until firm in the center or a skewer inserted into the middle comes out clean. Leave to cool in the tin for about 5 minutes, then turn out and cool on a wire rack. Dust with icing sugar.

• Per serving (for ten) 342 calories, protein 6g, carbohydrate 46g, fat 16g, saturated fat 2g, fiber 2g, added sugar 10g, salt 0.46g

Wonderfully moist and fruity, this cake is a snacktime favorite.

Raspberry and Blueberry Lime Drizzle Cake

8oz butter, softened
8oz golden caster sugar
4 eggs
9oz self-raising flour, sifted with a pinch of salt
grated zest and juice of 2 limes
1oz ground almonds
4oz each blueberries and raspberries

FOR THE SYRUP
8 tbsp lime juice (about 4 limes)
grated zest of 1 lime
5oz golden caster sugar

Takes 1 hour and 25 minutes •
Serves 12

1 Preheat oven to 350°F. Line the base and sides of a 8in square cake tin and butter the paper.

2 Cream the butter and sugar together until light. Gradually beat in the eggs, adding a little of the flour towards the end to prevent curdling. Beat in the lime zest, then fold in the rest of the flour and almonds. Fold in about 3 tablespoons of lime juice, giving a good dropping consistency. Fold in three quarters of the blueberries and raspberries and turn into the prepared tin. Smooth, then scatter the remaining fruit on top. Bake for about 1 hour or until firm.

3 Gently heat the lime juice, zest and sugar in a saucepan, without allowing to bubble. While the cake is still hot, prick it all over with a skewer then spoon the syrup over it.

• Per serving 370 calories, protein 5g, carbohydrate 49g, fat 19g, saturated fat 10g, fiber 1g, added sugar 32g, salt 0.61g

This cake is very moist and light, and the apricots add a juicy note –
a brilliant special-occasion dessert.

Almond Cake with Clementines

4oz ready-to-eat dried apricots
6fl oz clementine juice (about
6–8 clementines)
4oz butter, softened
4oz golden caster sugar
2 eggs
2oz self-raising flour
6oz ground almonds
½ tsp vanilla extract
2 tbsp slivered almonds
icing sugar, for dusting
8 clementines in syrup (from a jar),
to serve
thick cream or Greek yogurt,
to serve

Takes 1 hour 50 minutes • Serves 8

1 Preheat oven to 350°F. Butter and line the base of a 8in round cake tin. Finely chop the apricots and put in a pan with the clementine juice. Bring to a boil, then gently simmer for 5 minutes. Leave to cool.

2 Beat the butter, sugar, eggs and flour in a bowl for 2 minutes until light and fluffy, then fold in the ground almonds, vanilla and apricots along with their juices.

3 Turn the mixture into the prepared tin and smooth. Scatter the slivered almonds on top. Bake for 40–50 minutes until firm. Cool in the tin for 5 minutes, then turn out and cool on a wire rack. Dust the cake with icing sugar. Slice, and put a wedge on each plate with a clementine. Spoon the syrup over the cake and fruit. Serve with the cream or yogurt.

• Per serving 291 calories, protein 6g, carbohydrate 27g, fat 19g, saturated fat 8g, fiber 2g, added sugar 15g, salt 0.36g

Buy your mangos a couple of days ahead
to ensure they are fully ripe.

Mango, Banana and Coconut Cake

1 medium, ripe mango
2 ripe bananas
1 tsp vanilla extract
8oz butter, softened
5oz light muscovado sugar
2 eggs, beaten
2oz desiccated coconut
8oz self-raising flour
½ tsp bicarbonate of soda
1 tsp mixed spice

FOR THE FILLING
7oz packet full-fat cream cheese
2 tsp lemon juice
1oz icing sugar, plus extra for
dusting

Takes 55 minutes • Serves 10

1 Preheat oven 325°F. Butter and line the bases of two round 8in sandwich tins. Peel, stone and chop the mango, then purée the flesh. Mash the bananas, then mix in half the mango purée and the vanilla.

2 Beat together the butter and sugar until light and fluffy. Beat in the eggs, a little at a time, then stir in the banana mixture, and the coconut. Sift in the flour, bicarbonate of soda and spice, then fold in lightly. Divide the mixture between the tins and smooth. Bake for 30–35 minutes. Cool in the tins for 5 minutes, then turn out on to a wire rack.

3 Beat together the filling ingredients, then stir in the reserved mango. Spread one cake with the filling. Put the other cake on top and dust lightly with icing sugar.

• Per serving 468 calories, protein 5g, carbohydrate 42g, fat 32g, saturated fat 21g, fiber 2g, added sugar 17g, salt 0.83g

A perfect cake for Easter from Orlando Murrin,
editor of *Good Food Magazine*.

Lemon Flower Cake

FOR THE SUGAR-FROSTED FLOWERS
selection of pansies, calendulas and
other seasonal edible flowers
1 egg white, very lightly beaten
caster sugar, for coating the flowers

FOR THE CAKE
6oz butter, softened
6oz caster sugar
3 eggs
6oz self-raising flour
1½ tsp baking powder
finely grated zest of 1 lemon

FOR THE TOPPING AND FILLING
3oz caster sugar, plus extra for
sprinkling
juice of 1½ lemons
9oz tub mascarpone

Takes 50 minutes, plus 2 hours drying
time • Serves 8–10

1 Brush the flower petals with the egg white,
then sprinkle with the caster sugar. Shake off
any excess. Leave for 2 hours to dry.
2 Preheat oven to 375°F. Lightly butter and
line two 7in round sandwich tins. Put all the
cake ingredients in a large mixing bowl, add a
tablespoon of warm water and beat until
smooth. Divide the mixture between the tins,
smooth, then bake for 25–30 minutes until the
cakes spring back when pressed.
3 Mix the topping sugar with the juice of one
lemon. Prick the cakes and spoon the topping
mixture over. Cool, then transfer to a wire rack.
Add the remaining lemon juice to the
mascarpone and use this mixture to layer the
cakes. Sprinkle caster sugar lightly over the
top, then decorate with the flowers.

• Per serving (for eight) 538 calories, protein 6g,
carbohydrate 54g, fat 35g, saturated fat 21g, fiber 1g,
added sugar 35g, salt 1.12g

This treat can be stored in the fridge for up to 3 days.

Citrus Poppy Seed Cake

6oz butter, softened
6oz caster sugar
3 eggs, beaten
9oz self-raising flour
2oz poppy seeds
grated rind of 2 oranges
grated rind of 2 lemons
4 rounded tbsp natural yogurt

FOR THE TOPPING
9oz tub mascarpone
grated rind and juice of 1 small
orange
3 tbsp orange or lemon curd
grated rind of 1 lemon

Takes 1 hour 5 minutes • Serves 10

1 Preheat oven to 300°F. Butter and line the base of a deep 8in round cake tin. Using a wooden spoon, beat together the butter, sugar, eggs, flour, poppy seeds, citrus rinds and yogurt until smooth.
2 Spread the mixture in the tin and bake for 45–50 minutes until just firm. Cool in the tin for 10 minutes, then turn out and cool on a wire rack. Peel off the paper.
3 Meanwhile, mix the mascarpone with enough orange juice to make a spreadable icing. Lightly swirl in the curd to give a marbled effect. Roughly spread over the top and sides of the cake, and scatter the grated citrus rind over the top to decorate.

• Per serving 483 calories, protein 7g, carbohydrate 48g, fat 31g, saturated fat 11g, fiber 2g, added sugar 18g, salt 0.74g

An all-in-one cake, topped with fresh apples,
then glazed for a beautiful finish.

Apple Cake in a Nutshell

3 eggs
6oz butter, melted
12oz self-raising flour
2 tsp ground cinnamon
6oz light muscovado sugar
3 medium eating apples, such as
Cox's, unpeeled and cored
4oz dates, stoned and cut
into pieces
4oz blanched hazelnuts,
roughly chopped
3 tbsp apricot compote

Takes 1¼ hours • Serves 12

1 Preheat oven to 350°F. Butter and line the base of a 8in cake tin. Beat the eggs into the cooled butter. Put the flour, cinnamon and sugar into a separate bowl, and mix well.
2 Cut two of the apples into chunks. Stir the chunks into the flour with the dates and half of the hazelnuts. Mix well. Pour the egg and butter mixture into the flour mixture and stir gently. Spoon into the tin, and smooth.
3 Cut the remaining apple into thin slices and arrange over the cake. Sprinkle the remaining hazelnuts over the apple slices. Bake for 50 minutes–1 hour, or until a skewer inserted comes out clean. Cool in the tin for 5 minutes, then turn out on a wire rack. While the cake is still warm, heat the apricot compote. Brush over the cake, then cool completely.

• Per serving 377 calories, protein 6g, carbohydrate 49g, fat 19g, saturated fat 8g, fiber 3g, added sugar 15g, salt 0.61g

This unconventionally made bittersweet cake
freezes beautifully.

Orange and Almond Cake

1 medium orange
6oz butter, softened
6oz light muscovado sugar
3 eggs
6oz self-raising flour
½ tsp bicarbonate of soda
2oz ground almonds
icing sugar, for dredging

Takes 50 minutes • Serves 12

1 Preheat oven to 375°F. Butter and line the base of a 9in round deep cake tin. Cut the whole orange – skin, pith, flesh, the lot – into pieces. Remove any pits, then whiz the orange pieces in a food processor to a finely chopped purée.

2 Tip the butter, sugar, eggs, flour, bicarbonate of soda and almonds into the processor and whiz for 10 seconds, until smooth. Pour into the prepared tin and smooth the top.

3 Bake for 25–30 minutes, until the cake is risen and brown. Allow to cool in the tin for 5 minutes before turning out on to a wire rack. Dredge thickly with icing sugar before serving.

• Per serving 266 calories, protein 4g, carbohydrate 29g, fat 16g, saturated fat 8g, fiber 1g, added sugar 16g, salt 0.61g

These squares are really light, and delicious hot or cold.

Sour Cream Rhubarb Squares

4oz butter, softened
4oz golden caster sugar
4oz mixed nuts, roughly chopped
1 tsp ground cinnamon
9oz dark muscovado sugar
1 large egg
8oz plain flour
1 tsp bicarbonate of soda
½ tsp salt
2 x 4fl oz cartons sour cream
10oz rhubarb, cut into ½ in pieces

Takes 1 hour 20 minutes • Serves 15

1 Preheat oven to 350°F. Line a 13 x 9in deep baking tin with baking paper. Melt about ½oz of the butter and stir into the caster sugar, nuts and cinnamon in a bowl. Set aside.

2 Beat together the rest of the butter with the muscovado sugar and egg. When smooth and creamy, stir in the flour, bicarbonate of soda, salt and the sour cream. Lastly, stir in the rhubarb.

3 Pour the rhubarb mixture into the prepared tin and sprinkle with the sugar and nut topping. Bake for 30–35 minutes or until a skewer inserted in the center comes out clean. Serve immediately as a pudding, or leave to cool and cut into squares. Keeps for 4–5 days in an airtight tin.

• Per serving 277 calories, protein 4g, carbohydrate 37g, fat 13g, saturated fat 7g, fiber 1g, added sugar 24g, salt 0.63g

The perfect crumbly dessert for a summer
Sunday lunch or dinner.

Strawberry and Cinnamon Torte

6oz ground almonds
6oz butter, softened
6oz golden caster sugar
6oz self-raising flour
1 tsp ground cinnamon
1 egg, plus 1 egg yolk
1lb strawberries, hulled and
sliced
icing sugar, for dusting
whipped double cream mixed with
Greek yogurt, to serve

Takes 1¼ hours • Serves 6–8

1 Preheat oven to 350°F. Butter and line the base of a loose-bottomed 9in cake tin. In a food processor, mix the ground almonds, butter, sugar, flour, cinnamon, egg and egg yolk until evenly mixed.

2 Tip half the mixture in the tin, and smooth. Spread the strawberries on top. Top with the remaining cake mixture; spread smooth.

3 Bake for 1 hour–1 hour 5 minutes. Check after 40 minutes – if the torte is getting too brown, cover loosely with foil. When cooked, the torte should be slightly risen and dark golden brown.

4 Cool slightly, then remove from the tin. Slide on to a plate and dust with icing sugar. Serve warm, in wedges, with spoonfuls of cream and Greek yogurt.

• Per serving (for eight) 491 calories, protein 9g, carbohydrate 45g, fat 32g, saturated fat 13g, fiber 3g, added sugar 23g, salt 0.68g

Blueberries bake really well in cakes, as their purple skins keep in their juicy centers.

Blueberry Sour Cream Cake

6oz butter, softened
6oz golden caster sugar
3 large eggs
8oz self-raising flour
1 tsp baking powder
2 tsp vanilla extract
4fl oz carton sour cream
3 x 4½oz punnets blueberries

FOR THE FROSTING
7oz tub cream cheese (such as Philadelphia)
4oz icing sugar

Takes 1 hour 25 minutes • Serves 10

1 Preheat oven to 350°F. Butter and line the base of a 9in round cake tin. Put the butter, sugar, eggs, flour, baking powder and vanilla in a bowl. Beat for 2–3 minutes until pale and well mixed. Beat in 4 tablespoons sour cream, then stir in half the blueberries.
2 Tip the mixture into the tin and level. Bake for 50 minutes, or until it feels firm to the touch and springs back when lightly pressed. Cool for 10 minutes, then take out of the tin and peel off the paper. Leave to finish cooling.
3 Beat the cream cheese with the icing sugar and the remaining sour cream until smooth and creamy. Spread over the top of the cooled cake and scatter with the remaining blueberries. The cake will keep in the fridge for a couple of days.

• Per serving 469 calories, protein 6g, carbohydrate 50g, fat 29g, saturated fat 17g, fiber 1g, added sugar 29g, salt 0.93g

This tasty cake can be made in advance, but is best eaten within 2–3 days.

Raspberry and Almond Madeira Cake

6oz butter, softened
6oz caster sugar
1 tsp vanilla extract
3 eggs, lightly beaten
2oz flaked almonds
grated zest of 1 orange
4oz plain flour, sifted
4oz self-raising flour, sifted
2 tbsp milk
8oz raspberries, fresh or frozen
icing sugar, for dusting

Takes 1½ hours • Serves 8

1 Preheat oven to 325°F. Line a deep 8in cake tin. Cream the butter and sugar. Beat in the vanilla, then gradually beat in the eggs.
2 Set aside a few almonds. Crumble the rest and stir them and the zest into the batter. Fold in the sifted flours and milk, then fold in all but eight of the raspberries.
3 Put the mixture in the tin and level, then arrange the remaining raspberries on top. Sprinkle the remaining almonds over the top, and bake for 1 hour 15 minutes. Cool in the tin for 10 minutes, then cool on a rack. Dust with icing sugar.

• Per serving 410 calories, protein 7g, carbohydrate 45g, fat 24g, saturated fat 12g, fiber 2g, added sugar 24g, salt 0.61g

The juicy flavour of a whole orange goes into this cake.

Whole Orange Cake

1 small orange
5oz caster sugar
3 eggs
3oz self-raising flour
4oz ground almonds
2oz butter, melted

FOR THE ICING
3oz icing sugar
juice of 1 small sweet orange (or
enough to make a smooth
pouring icing)
crème fraîche, to serve (optional)

Takes 1 hour 45 minutes •
Serves 8–10

1 Put the orange in a pan and cover with cold water. Bring to a boil, cover and simmer for 1 hour. Remove the orange and cool.
2 Preheat oven to 350°F. Butter and line the base of a 8in round, deep cake tin. Roughly chop the cooked orange, discarding the pits. Whiz in a food processor until smooth. Whisk the sugar and eggs until light and fluffy.
3 Sift the flour and ground almonds on to the egg mixture. Using a large metal spoon, fold gently, then add the orange purée and melted butter. Fold in gently until just mixed. Pour the cake mixture into the prepared tin. Bake for 40–45 minutes until the cake is brown and springs back when lightly pressed. Cool in the tin for 5 minutes. Mix the icing sugar and juice together, drizzle, and serve with crème fraîche.

• Per serving (for eight) 307 calories, protein 6g, carbohydrate 41g, fat 14g, saturated fat 4g, fiber 2g, added sugar 30g, salt 0.29g

Made with ground almonds and dark chocolate, this flourless cake is beautifully dark, rich and moist.

Seriously Rich Chocolate Cake

4oz butter, diced
5oz best-quality dark chocolate, broken into pieces
6 eggs, separated
5oz ground almonds
1 tbsp kirsch or Cointreau (optional)
3oz caster sugar
cocoa powder, for dusting
crème fraîche, to serve

Takes 55 minutes • Serves 8–10

1 Preheat oven to 340ºF. Butter and line the base of a 9in springform cake tin. Dust the sides with a little flour. Melt the butter and chocolate, stir until smooth, and leave for about 5 minutes to cool slightly. Stir in the egg yolks, ground almonds, and the liqueur, if using.
2 Put the egg whites into a bowl, add a pinch of salt and whisk until soft peaks form. Continue whisking, sprinkling in the sugar a little at a time, until stiff peaks form. Stir 2 tablespoons of the whites into the chocolate mixture, then carefully fold in the remainder.
3 Spoon the mixture into the prepared tin and bake for 30–35 minutes until well risen and just firm. Cool in the tin. Remove the cake and peel away the paper. Dust with cocoa powder, slice, and serve with crème fraîche.

• Per serving (for eight) 401 calories, protein 10g, carbohydrate 24g, fat 30g, saturated fat 11g, fiber 2g, added sugar 22g, salt 0.66g

Chocolate and orange is a classic combination.

Dark Chocolate and Orange Cake

1 Seville orange
3 eggs
10oz caster sugar
8½fl oz sunflower oil
4oz dark chocolate, broken
into pieces and melted
1oz cocoa powder
9oz plain flour
1½ tsp baking powder

FOR THE CHOCOLATE GANACHE
8oz dark chocolate, broken
into pieces
1 cup heavy cream
candied orange zest, to decorate

Takes 2 hours 10 minutes,
plus 1½ hours cooling time •
Serves 10

1 Pierce the orange with a skewer. Cook in a pan of boiling water for 30 minutes. Remove and whiz the whole orange in a food processor. Discard any pits and cool.
2 Preheat oven to 350°F. Butter and line the base of a 9in round cake tin. Lightly beat the eggs, sugar and oil. Gradually beat in the puréed orange and cooled, melted chocolate. Sift in the cocoa, flour and baking powder. Mix well and pour into the tin. Bake for 55–60 minutes. Cool for 10 minutes, then turn out on to a wire rack.
3 Put the ganache chocolate into a heatproof bowl. Boil the cream in a pan, pour over the chocolate, and stir until smooth. Cool, up to 1½ hours, until firm. Spread over the cake, and decorate with the candied zest.

• Per serving 703 calories, protein 7g, carbohydrate 73g, fat 45g, saturated fat 16g, fiber 2g, added sugar 51g, salt 0.42g

Moist and fruity enough to serve warm with cream,
but just as good cold.

Pear, Hazelnut and Chocolate Cake

4oz blanched hazelnuts
5oz self-raising flour
6oz butter, cut into small
pieces
5oz golden caster sugar
2 large eggs, beaten
5 small ripe Conference pears
2oz dark chocolate, chopped
into small chunks
2 tbsp apricot jam

Takes 1½ hours • Serves 8

1 Preheat oven to 325°F. Butter and line the base of a 8in round cake tin. Grind the hazelnuts in a food processor until fairly fine. Add the flour and mix briefly. Add the butter and pulse until it forms crumbs. Add the sugar and eggs and mix briefly. Peel, core and chop two of the pears. Stir the pears and chocolate lightly into the cake mixture.
2 Spoon the mixture into the prepared tin and smooth the top. Peel, core and slice the remaining pears and scatter over the top of the cake. Press down lightly and bake for 50–60 minutes, until firm to the touch. Cool in the tin for 10 minutes, then turn out and cool on a wire rack. Warm the jam and brush over the top. Serve warm or cold.

• Per serving 470 calories, protein 6g, carbohydrate 47g, fat 30g, saturated fat 14g, fiber 3g, added sugar 18g, salt 0.5g

Rich with brandy-steeped prunes, this is a cake
for real lovers of chocolate.

Prune and Chocolate Torte

9oz no-soak prunes, halved
4 tbsp brandy
1oz cocoa powder
4oz dark chocolate (at least
70% cocoa solids), broken into
pieces
2oz butter
6oz golden caster sugar
4 large egg whites
3oz plain flour
1 tsp ground cinnamon
lightly whipped cream, or crème
fraîche, to serve

Takes 1 hour 5 minutes,
plus 30 minutes soaking time •
Serves 8

1 Soak the prunes in brandy for about
30 minutes. Preheat oven to 375°F. Butter a
9in loose-bottomed cake tin. Put the cocoa,
chocolate, butter and 5oz of the sugar
in a pan, add 3½fl oz hot water and gently heat
until smooth. Leave to cool slightly.
2 Whisk the egg whites to soft peaks, then
gradually whisk in the remaining sugar. Sift
the flour and cinnamon over and gently fold
in with a metal spoon, until almost combined.
Add the chocolate mixture and fold in until
evenly combined.
3 Pour the mixture into the tin and arrange
the prunes over the top. Sprinkle over any
remaining brandy and bake for about
30 minutes until just firm. Serve with cream
or crème fraîche.

• Per serving 311 calories, protein 5g, carbohydrate
51g, fat 10g, saturated fat 6g, fiber 3g, added sugar
31g, salt 0.18g

A special treat for dessert or snack.

Almond and Chocolate Torte with Apricot Cream

5 egg whites
8oz golden caster sugar
4oz ground almonds
2oz toasted flaked almonds
2oz dark chocolate, chopped

FOR THE APRICOT CREAM
1½ cups heavy cream
12oz apricot compote

FOR THE DECORATION
3 tbsp toasted flaked almonds
1oz dark chocolate, shaved
icing sugar, for dusting

Takes 1 hour 5 minutes • Serves 8–12

1 Preheat oven to 350°F. Butter and line the base of a deep 10in cake tin. Whisk the egg whites until stiff, then gradually whisk in the golden caster sugar, a tablespoonful at a time.
2 Lightly fold in the ground almonds, the toasted flaked almonds and the chopped chocolate. Pour the mixture into the cake tin and bake for 40–45 minutes until crisp on top and light golden. Allow to cool in the tin for 5 minutes, then turn out and leave to cool on a wire rack.
3 Whip the cream until it just holds its shape. Spoon in the apricot compote, then fold it in gently to create swirls of apricot. Spoon over the torte and sprinkle with toasted flaked almonds and chocolate shavings. Dust lightly with sifted icing sugar.

• Per serving (for eight) 574 calories, protein 9g, carbohydrate 44g, fat 42g, saturated fat 18g, fiber 3g, added sugar 37g, salt 0.16g

Scatter over a handful of little chocolate eggs for an Easter treat.

Chocca Mocca Caramel Cake

2 tsp instant coffee granules/powder
2 tbsp cocoa
6oz butter, softened
6oz golden caster sugar
2 eggs
2 tbsp golden syrup
8oz self-raising flour
4 tbsp milk
2 x 1¾oz chocolate caramel bars,
broken into pieces

FOR THE ICING
2 x 1¾oz chocolate caramel bars,
broken into pieces
2oz butter
2 tbsp milk
4oz icing sugar, sifted

Takes 1½ hours • Serves 10–12

1 Preheat oven to 180°F. Butter and line the base of an 8in round cake tin. Mix the coffee, cocoa and 2 tablespoons hot water to a smooth paste. Put the butter, sugar, eggs, syrup, flour, milk and cocoa paste in a bowl and beat for 2–3 minutes until smooth. Stir the caramel bar pieces into the mixture.
2 Turn the mixture into the prepared tin and smooth. Bake for 50–60 minutes, until the top springs back when you press it lightly. Cool in the tin for 5 minutes, then turn out, peel off the lining paper and leave to cool.
3 For the icing, gently heat the caramel bar pieces, butter and milk until smooth, stirring all the time, then remove from the heat and stir in the icing sugar. Leave to cool. Spread the icing over the top of the cooled cake.

• Per serving (for ten) 474 calories, protein 5g, carbohydrate 59g, fat 26g, saturated fat 15g, fiber 1g, added sugar 43g, salt 0.8g

These moist little squares are deliciously chocolatey without being sickly.

Chocolate Cinnamon Crumb Squares

FOR THE CRUMBLE TOPPING
2oz plain flour
1 tbsp cocoa powder
2 tsp ground cinnamon
2oz light muscovado sugar
2oz butter, cut into pieces

FOR THE CAKE
8oz dark chocolate, broken into pieces
6oz butter, softened
8oz light muscovado sugar
3 eggs
6oz self-raising flour
icing sugar, for dusting

Takes 2 hours • Makes 16

1 Preheat oven to 340°F. Butter and line the base and sides of an 8in square cake tin. For the topping, put the flour, cocoa, cinnamon, sugar and the butter into a food processor, then pulse until the mixture forms a crumble. Set aside.

2 For the cake, put the chocolate in a bowl and melt in the microwave on Medium for 2–3 minutes. Put the butter, sugar, eggs and flour in a bowl and beat for 2–3 minutes, until well mixed. Stir in the chocolate until it is evenly mixed in.

3 Tip the mixture into the tin and smooth. Sprinkle the crumble evenly over the top. Bake for 50–60 minutes, until a skewer inserted comes out clean. Leave to cool for 10 minutes in the tin, then turn out to cool on a wire rack. Dust the top lightly with icing sugar.

• Per square 298 calories, protein 3g, carbohydrate 36g, fat 16g, saturated fat 10g, fiber 1g, added sugar 25g, salt 0.43g

This brownie, bulging with chunks of chocolate
and nuts, is perfect for lunchboxes.

Chunky Chocolate Nut Brownies

8oz oats
1oz desiccated coconut
5oz butter, cut into pieces
2oz light muscovado sugar
5 tbsp golden syrup
4oz brazil nuts (or cashews),
cut into large chunks
2oz almonds, cut into large
chunks
3oz good-quality dark
chocolate, broken into
large pieces

Takes 45 minutes • Makes 12

1 Preheat oven to 350ºF. Lightly butter a 9in square tin and line the base. Mix together the oats and coconut.

2 Put the butter, sugar and syrup in a pan, cook over a low heat, stirring occasionally, until the butter has melted and the sugar dissolved. Remove from the heat and stir in the oat and coconut mixture. Spoon into the tin and press down evenly. Scatter over the nuts and press lightly into the mixture. Stick the chunks of chocolate between the nuts. Bake for 25–30 minutes, or until a pale golden color.

3 Mark into bars or squares with the back of a knife while still warm, then allow to cool completely before cutting through and removing from the tin.

• Per brownie 325 calories, protein 5g, carbohydrate 28g, fat 22g, saturated fat 10g, fiber 2g, added sugar 15g, salt 0.3g

Deliciously moist, chocolatey and utterly irresistible – they'll keep for up to a week, tightly wrapped in foil.

Banana Nut Brownies

6oz butter, cut into pieces
10oz light muscovado sugar
6oz dark chocolate, broken into pieces
4oz bag nuts, toasted and chopped
3 eggs, beaten
2 ripe bananas, mashed
4oz self-raising flour
2 tbsp cocoa powder
1 tsp baking powder

Takes 50 minutes • Makes 15

1 Preheat oven to 350ºF. Butter and line an 7 x 11in Swiss roll tin with baking paper. Put the butter, sugar and chocolate in a large pan and heat gently, stirring, until melted and smooth, then remove the pan from the heat.

2 Stir in the nuts, eggs and bananas until well mixed, then sift in the flour, cocoa and baking powder.

3 Pour the mixture into the tin and bake for 30 minutes until firm in the center. Cool in the tin, then turn out and cut into 15 squares.

• Per brownie 336 calories, protein 5g, carbohydrate 37g, fat 20g, saturated fat 9g, fiber 1g, added sugar 28g, salt 0.5g

This no-bake treat is great for lunchboxes.

Choc Crunchies

8oz digestive biscuits
4oz butter
3 tbsp golden syrup
2 tbsp cocoa powder
2oz raisins
4oz dark chocolate

Takes 50 minutes • Serves 8–10

1 Butter an 7in sandwich tin. Seal the biscuits in a strong polythene bag and bash into uneven crumbs with a rolling pin.
2 Melt the butter and syrup in a pan (or microwave on High for about 1½ minutes). Stir in the cocoa and raisins, then thoroughly stir in the biscuit crumbs. Spoon into the tin and press down firmly.
3 Melt the chocolate in a heatproof bowl over a pan of simmering water (or microwave on Medium for 2–3 minutes). Spread over the biscuit base and chill for about half an hour. Keeps for up to 1 week wrapped in foil.

• Per serving (for eight) 327 calories, protein 3g, carbohydrate 36g, fat 20g, saturated fat 11g, fiber 1g, added sugar 17g, salt 0.77g

These little squares are a tempting combination of chewy marshmallows and crunchy nuts, coated with chocolate.

Rocky Road Squares

18oz milk or dark chocolate, broken into pieces
10 marshmallows, cut into small pieces
3oz pecans, almonds or walnuts (or a mixture), roughly chopped

Takes 15 minutes, plus 2 hours cooling • Makes 50

1 Line a shallow 8in square cake tin with baking paper. In a heatproof bowl set over a pan of simmering water, gently melt the chocolate, then stir in the marshmallows and nuts, mixing well.

2 Pour the mixture into the tin and smooth the top. Leave to set for about 2 hours. Dip a sharp knife in hot water and wipe; cut the cooled mixture into 1in squares.

• Per square 67 calories, protein 1g, carbohydrate 7g, fat 4g, saturated fat 2g, fiber trace, added sugar 5g, salt 0.02g

These irresistible bars can be frozen, unfrosted,
for up to 2 months.

Cappuccino Bars

1 tsp cocoa powder, plus extra
for dusting
2 rounded tbsp coffee granules
8oz butter, softened
8oz caster sugar
4 eggs
8oz self-raising flour
1 tsp baking powder

FOR THE WHITE CHOCOLATE
FROSTING
4oz white chocolate, broken
into pieces
2oz butter, softened
3 tbsp milk
6oz icing sugar

Takes 50 minutes • Makes 24

1 Preheat oven to 350°F. Butter and line the
bottom of a shallow 11 x 7in oblong tin. Mix
the cocoa and coffee granules into 2
tablespoons warm water. Put in a large bowl
with the other cake ingredients.
2 Whisk for about 2 minutes with an electric
hand blender to combine, then tip into the
tin and level out. Bake for 35–40 minutes
until risen and firm to the touch. Cool in the
tin for 10 minutes, then cool on a rack. Peel
off the paper.
3 For the frosting, melt the chocolate, butter
and milk in a bowl over a pan of simmering
water. Remove the bowl and sift in the icing
sugar. Beat until smooth, then spread over the
cake. Finish with a dusting of cocoa powder.
Cut into 24 bars.

• Per bar 219 calories, protein 3g, carbohydrate 27g,
fat 12g, saturated fat 6g, fiber trace, added sugar 19g,
salt 0.43g

Unrefined dark muscovado sugar gives these brownies
a sticky toffee flavor.

Toffee Brownies

12oz dark chocolate
(preferably around 50–60% cocoa
solids), broken into pieces
9oz unsalted butter, cut
into pieces
3 large eggs
9oz dark muscovado sugar
3oz plain flour
1 tsp baking powder

Takes 1 hour 5 minutes, plus 1 hour
cooling • Makes 16

1 Preheat oven to 325°F. Butter and line the base of a shallow 9in square cake tin. Melt the chocolate and butter together, then stir well and cool.

2 Whisk the eggs until pale, then whisk in the sugar until thick and glossy and well combined. Gently fold in the melted chocolate mixture, then sift in the flour and baking powder and gently stir until smooth.

3 Pour into the prepared cake tin and bake for 30–35 minutes, or until firm to the touch. Test by inserting a wooden cocktail stick into the middle – there should be a few moist crumbs sticking to it. The mixture will still be soft in the center, but will firm up on cooling.

4 Cool in the tin on a wire rack for at least 1 hour, then cut into 16 squares and finish cooling on the rack.

• Per brownie 324 calories, protein 3g, carbohydrate 34g, fat 20g, saturated fat 12g, fiber 1g, added sugar 30g, salt 0.14g

A treat for tea by the fire, this afternoon bake keeps moist,
well-wrapped, for 4–5 days.

Mincemeat and Marzipan Teabread

8oz self-raising flour
4oz cold butter, cut into pieces
3oz light muscovado sugar
3oz marzipan, cut into ½in cubes
2 eggs
10oz mincemeat
2 tbsp flaked almonds
icing sugar, for dusting (optional)

Takes 1 hour 20 minutes • Serves 12

1 Preheat oven to 350ºF. Butter a 2lb loaf tin and line the base with greaseproof paper. Tip the flour into a bowl, add the cold butter and rub until the mixture forms fine crumbs. Stir in the sugar and marzipan cubes.
2 In another bowl, lightly whisk the eggs, then stir in the mincemeat. Stir this into the flour mixture until evenly combined. Spoon into the prepared loaf tin, smooth, and sprinkle the flaked almonds over the top. Bake for 1 hour until the teabread is risen and golden brown, or a skewer inserted comes out clean. Lightly dust the teabread with icing sugar while it is still hot.
3 Allow to cool in the tin for 10 minutes, then tip on to a wire rack to cool completely. Peel off the lining paper and cut into slices – it's also very good spread with butter.

• Per serving 265 calories, protein 4g, carbohydrate 41g, fat 11g, saturated fat 5g, fiber 1g, added sugar 15g, salt 0.44g

The natural sweetness provided by the bananas helps reduce the amount of sugar that needs to be used.

Banana Teabread

6oz plain wholemeal flour
2oz medium oatmeal
4oz butter, softened
4oz dark muscovado sugar
2 tsp baking powder
¼ tsp ground cinnamon
2 eggs, beaten
3–4 ripe bananas, about 12oz, peeled and mashed
4oz walnuts, roughly chopped

Takes 1 hour 35 minutes • Serves 10

1 Preheat oven to 350ºF. Butter and line the base of a 2lb loaf tin with baking paper. Put the wholemeal flour, oatmeal, butter, sugar, baking powder, cinnamon and eggs into a large bowl and, using an electric hand whisk, beat together until evenly mixed. Stir in the bananas and walnuts, taking care not to overmix.

2 Spoon the mixture into the prepared tin and bake for 1¼ hours or until a skewer inserted comes out clean (cover the cake with foil halfway through cooking to prevent the top from overbrowning). Allow the cake to cool in the tin for 5 minutes, then carefully turn out, peel off the lining paper and cool completely on a wire rack.

• Per serving 309 calories, protein 6g, carbohydrate 34g, fat 17g, saturated fat 3g, fiber 3g, added sugar 10g, salt 0.53g

Choose a richly flavored Greek or Mexican honey
for an extra-special taste.

Walnut, Date and Honey Cake

8oz self-raising flour
½ tsp ground cinnamon
6oz butter, softened
4oz light muscovado sugar
3 tbsp clear honey
2 eggs, beaten
2 medium, ripe bananas, about
9oz total weight
in their skins
4oz pitted dates
2oz pack walnut pieces

Takes 1 hour 25 minutes •
Serves 8–10

1 Preheat oven to 325°F. Line the base and long sides of a 2lb loaf tin with greaseproof paper, buttering the tin and paper. Tip the flour, cinnamon, butter, sugar, 2 tablespoons of the honey and the eggs into a large mixing bowl. Mash the bananas and chop the dates (kitchen scissors are easiest for this), and add to the bowl. Beat the mixture for 2–3 minutes, using a wooden spoon or hand-held mixer, until well blended.

2 Spoon into the prepared tin and smooth. Scatter the walnut pieces over the top. Bake for 1 hour, then lightly press the top – it should feel firm. If not, bake for an additional 10 minutes.

3 Cool for 15 minutes, then lift out of the tin using the paper. When cold, drizzle the remaining honey over. Cut into thick slices.

• Per serving (for eight) 440 calories, protein 6g, carbohydrate 54g, fat 24g, saturated fat 13g, fiber 1.5g, added sugar 25g, salt 0.7g

Measuring the ingredients in a jug makes this really easy to throw together – though it does need to be started the day before baking.

Peach and Cherry Teabread

1 cup ready-to-eat dried peaches, chopped
½ cup undyed glacé cherries, halved
½ cup raisins
1 cup light muscovado sugar
1 cup freshly made hot tea
1 egg, beaten
1 pint self-raising flour
1 tsp ground cinnamon
icing sugar, for dusting

Takes 1¾ hours, plus overnight soaking • Serves 12–14

1 Put the fruit and sugar in a bowl, pour over the tea and stir well. Cover with a tea towel and leave overnight for the fruit to plump up.

2 Preheat oven to 325°F. Butter and line the base of a 2lb loaf tin with greaseproof paper. Stir the egg into the steeped fruit mixture, then sift in the flour and cinnamon. Mix well, then turn into the prepared tin and smooth the top.

3 Bake for 1¼–1½ hours until the teabread is risen and golden. Test with a skewer (it should come out clean). Cool in the tin for 10 minutes, then turn out and cool on a wire rack. Dust the top with icing sugar.

• Per serving (for twelve) 297 calories, protein 4g, carbohydrate 71g, fat 1g, saturated fat 0.4g, fiber 3g, added sugar 31g, salt 0.31g

Made in a flash, this is best cut into thick slices
and spread with butter while still warm.

Spotted Dog

10oz plain flour
½ tsp salt
1 tsp baking soda
3 tbsp caster sugar
4oz mixed dried fruit
1 egg, beaten
7fl oz buttermilk

Takes 50 minutes • Serves 10–12

1 Preheat oven to 375°F. Butter a 2lb loaf tin. Sift the flour, salt and bicarbonate of soda into a mixing bowl. Stir in the sugar, make a well in the center and add the dried fruit, egg and buttermilk. Mix lightly and quickly into the flour for a soft dough.
2 Using floured hands, remove the dough from the bowl and knead very briefly. Then press the dough into the prepared tin. Bake for 35–40 minutes until the top is a dark golden color and the loaf feels firm to the touch. Turn out and leave to cool. Serve thickly sliced and buttered.

• Per serving (for ten) 163 calories, protein 4g, carbohydrate 36g, fat 1g, saturated fat 0.3g, fiber 1g, added sugar 5g, salt 0.66g

Use a chunky marmalade to give this loaf extra
texture and a pretty top.

Sticky Marmalade Tealoaf

5oz marmalade (about
one third of a 15oz jar)
6oz butter, softened
6oz light muscovado sugar
3 eggs, beaten
8oz self-raising flour
½ tsp baking powder
2 tsp ground ginger
1 tsp mixed spice
4oz packet pecan halves

Takes 1½ hours • Serves 12

1 Preheat oven to 350°F. Butter a 2lb
loaf tin and line with greaseproof paper. Set
aside 1 tablespoon of the marmalade in a
small pan. In a bowl, blend the remaining
marmalade, butter, sugar, eggs, flour, baking
powder and spices for 1–2 minutes until
smooth and light. Stir in about three quarters
of the pecans.
2 Tip into the prepared tin and smooth the
top. Sprinkle with the reserved pecans. Bake
for about 1–1¼ hours until a skewer inserted
comes out clean. Cover loosely with foil after
40 minutes. Once cooked, carefully remove
from the tin, and cool slightly on a wire rack.
3 Gently heat the reserved marmalade,
stirring until it's smooth, and spread the glaze
over the top of the warm loaf. Serve in slices.

• Per serving 339 calories, protein 4g, carbohydrate
40g, fat 20g, saturated fat 8g, fiber 1g, added sugar
24g, salt 0.56g

Moist and irresistible, this rich cake has the most
wonderful, crunchy sugarplum topping.

Autumn Plum Crunch Cake

2 eggs, plus 1 egg yolk
5oz butter, softened
5oz golden caster sugar
5oz self-raising flour
grated zest and juice of 1 orange
8oz plums, pitted, half
roughly chopped into pieces
and half cut into wedges

FOR THE TOPPING
1½ tbsp fresh lemon juice
8oz golden caster sugar
1oz rough sugar pieces
(or sugar cubes), roughly
crushed

Takes 1½ hours • Serves 10

1 Preheat oven to 325°F. Butter and line the base of a 2lb loaf tin. Lightly beat the eggs and egg yolk with a pinch of salt.
2 Beat the butter and sugar in a bowl until light and fluffy. Pour in the eggs a little at a time, beating well after each addition. Fold in the flour with the orange zest and two tablespoons of the juice, then fold in the roughly chopped plums. Spoon into the prepared tin and scatter the plum wedges over. Bake for 50 minutes or until a skewer inserted comes out clean.
3 Cool for 10 minutes, then turn out on a wire rack. Mix the remaining orange juice with the lemon juice and caster sugar. Spoon over the cooling cake and sprinkle with the crushed sugar pieces. Cool until set.

• Per serving 327 calories, protein 3g, carbohydrate 51g, fat 14g, saturated fat 8g, fiber 1g, added sugar 38g, salt 0.45g

Although a fast and easy recipe,
this loaf is best made a day or two in advance.

Date and Walnut Tea Loaf

8oz pitted dates, chopped
1 tsp baking soda
4oz butter, cut into pieces
10oz self-raising flour, sifted
2oz chopped walnuts
4oz dark muscovado sugar
1 egg, beaten
2 tbsp demerara sugar

Takes 1 hour 40 minutes, plus cooling time • Serves 10–12

1 Mix the dates and bicarbonate of soda in a large bowl with a pinch of salt. Pour in 1 cup hot water, stir well and leave until cold. Preheat oven to 350°F. Butter a 2lb loaf tin and line the base and two long sides.
2 Rub the butter pieces into the flour until the mixture resembles coarse breadcrumbs. Stir in the walnuts and muscovado sugar until evenly combined.
3 Tip the flour mixture and the egg into the cooled dates. Beat well to mix, then pour into the prepared tin and sprinkle the demerara sugar on top. Bake in the oven for 1–1¼ hours or until a skewer come out clean. Cool in the tin for 5 minutes, then turn it out on to a wire rack. Double-wrap the cooled cake, and store in an airtight container for 1–2 days before eating.

• Per serving (for ten) 317 calories, protein 5g, carbohydrate 49g, fat 13g, saturated fat 6g, fiber 2g, added sugar 14g, salt 0.9g

The pumpkin adds a depth of flavor, a certain sweetness
and a lusciously moist texture.

Pumpkin and Ginger Teabread

6oz butter, melted
5oz clear honey
1 large egg, beaten
9oz raw peeled pumpkin or
butternut squash, coarsely
grated (about 1lb 2oz before
peeling and seeding)
4oz light muscovado sugar
12oz self-raising flour
1 tbsp ground ginger
2 tbsp demerara sugar, plus extra
for sprinkling (optional)

Takes 1½ hours • Serves 10

1 Preheat oven to 350°F. Butter and line the base and two long sides of a 2lb loaf tin with a strip of baking paper.
2 Mix the butter, honey and egg and stir in the pumpkin or squash. Then mix in the sugar, flour and ginger.
3 Pour into the prepared tin and sprinkle the top with the 2 tablespoons of demerara sugar. Bake for 50–60 minutes, until risen and golden brown. Leave in the tin for 5 minutes, then turn out and cool on a wire rack. Sprinkle more demerara sugar over the warm cake, if you wish. Serve thickly sliced and buttered.

• Per serving 351 calories, protein 4g, carbohydrate 52g, fat 15g, saturated fat 9g, fiber 1g, added sugar 24g, salt 0.69g

Try other fruits when in season – raspberries
and tayberries would be good.

Blackberry and Apple Loaf

9oz self-raising flour
6oz butter
6oz light muscovado sugar
½ tsp cinnamon
2 rounded tbsp demerara sugar
1 small eating apple, unpeeled,
coarsely grated down to the core
2 large eggs, beaten
finely grated zest of 1 orange
1 tsp baking powder
8oz blackberries

Takes 2 hours • Serves 10

1 Preheat oven to 350°F. Butter and line the base of a 2lb loaf tin. Rub the flour, butter and muscovado sugar together to make fine crumbs. Reserve 5 tablespoons of this mixture for the topping, and mix into it the cinnamon and demerara sugar. Set aside.
2 Mix the apple in with the eggs and the zest. Stir the baking powder into the rubbed-in mixture, then quickly and lightly stir in the egg mixture. Don't overmix.
3 Gently fold in three quarters of the berries. Spoon into the tin and level. Scatter the rest of the berries on top. Sprinkle over the topping and bake for 1 hour 20 minutes, testing with a skewer. After 50 minutes, cover loosely with foil. Leave in the tin for 30 minutes, then cool on a wire rack.

• Per serving 327 calories, protein 4g, carbohydrate 44g, fat 16g, saturated fat 10g, fiber 2g, added sugar 23g, salt 0.77g

Sealed in a plastic food bag, this loaf will freeze
for up to 3 months.

Banana and Walnut Tea Loaf

4oz butter, softened
5oz light muscovado sugar
2 eggs, lightly beaten
4oz walnuts, chopped
2 ripe bananas, mashed
2 tbsp milk
8oz self-raising flour

Takes 1¼ hours • Serves 12

1 Preheat oven to 350°F. Butter and line a
2lb loaf tin. Cream the butter and sugar, then
add the eggs. Set aside 1oz walnuts, then
fold the rest into the creamed mixture with
the bananas and milk. Fold in the flour.
Spoon into the tin and sprinkle over the
reserved walnuts.
2 Bake for 55–60 minutes until risen. Stand
for 10 minutes, then turn out, remove the
lining paper and cool.

• Per serving 267 calories, protein 4g, carbohydrate
33g, fat 14g, saturated fat 5g, fiber 1g, added sugar
12g, salt 0.37g

Unrefined caster sugar and a salted or slightly salted
creamy butter will give the best flavor.

Shortbread

6oz plain flour
4oz slightly salted butter, cut
into pieces and softened
2oz golden caster sugar
caster sugar, for sprinkling

Takes 50 minutes • Serves 8

1 Preheat oven to 300°F. Put the flour in a mixing bowl, add the butter and rub together to make fine crumbs. Stir in the sugar.
2 Work the mixture together until it forms a ball. Turn out on to a work surface and knead briefly until smooth. Roll and pat out on a very lightly floured surface to an 7in round. Smooth the surface with your hands. Carefully slide the dough on to an ungreased baking sheet and flute the edges. Mark the circle into eight triangles with a knife, not cutting all the way through. Prick the surface all over with a fork.
3 Bake for 30–35 minutes or until cooked. The shortbread should be very pale. While still warm, cut through the markings and sprinkle with caster sugar. Cool before eating.

• Per serving 186 calories, protein 2g, carbohydrate 22g, fat 10g, saturated fat 7g, fiber 1g, added sugar 8g, salt trace

Buttermilk adds a lightness that milk alone
won't give you.

Buttermilk Scones

12oz self-raising flour
4oz caster sugar
3oz butter, cut into small pieces
about 3¼ cup buttermilk or
natural low-fat yogurt
whipped cream and strawberry jam,
to serve

Takes 25 minutes • Makes 12

1 Preheat oven to 400°F. Mix together the flour and sugar in a bowl. Rub the butter in with your fingertips until the mixture resembles fine breadcrumbs. Make a well in the center of the ingredients and tip in the buttermilk, all at once, then mix lightly to form a soft dough.

2 Tip the dough out on to a lightly floured surface and knead briefly. Press the dough out to a 1in thickness, then stamp out 2in rounds with a cutter. Gather up the trimmings, knead again briefly and stamp out more rounds.

3 Transfer the buttermilk scones to a baking sheet, spaced a little apart, and bake for 12–15 minutes until risen and light golden. Leave the scones to cool on a wire rack and serve with the whipped cream and jam.

• Per scone 187 calories, protein 3g, carbohydrate 32g, fat 6g, saturated fat 4g, fiber 1g, added sugar 9g, salt 0.42g

These light and luscious tarts are a cross between the traditional Yorkshire curd tart and the lemony Portuguese version.

Cinnamon and Lemon Tarts with Berries

13oz pack ready-rolled puff pastry
7oz pack light cream cheese
grated rind of ½ lemon
4oz caster sugar
2 egg yolks
1 tbsp plain flour

TO SERVE
4oz each of raspberries and blueberries
cinnamon and icing sugar, for dusting
½ cup light cream (optional)

Takes 45 minutes • Serves 6

1 Preheat oven to 400ºF. Unwrap the pastry, then roll it out so you can stamp out 12 rounds using an 3in fluted cutter. Line 12 bun tins with the pastry and prick them with a fork all over (this is essential to stop the pastry rising up in the center and tipping the filling out).

2 Beat the cream cheese until soft, then beat in the lemon rind, sugar and egg yolks. Sift in the flour and mix well. Pour into the pastry cases, almost to the top.

3 Bake the tarts for 12–15 minutes, until the pastry is golden and the filling lightly colored. Carefully remove from the tins and leave aside on a rack to cool. To serve, place 2 tarts on a plate, scatter the berries over, dust lightly with cinnamon and icing sugar, then drizzle with a little cream, if you like.

• Per serving 411 calories, protein 8g, carbohydrate 48g, fat 22g, saturated fat 1g, fiber 1g, added sugar 19g, salt 0.76g

Decorated with ready-made writing icing and tiny sugar flowers, these little cakes couldn't be easier.

Mother's Day Fairy Cakes

FOR THE CAKES
6oz caster sugar
6oz butter, softened
3 eggs, beaten
6oz self-raising flour
1 tsp baking powder

FOR THE DECORATION
5oz icing sugar, sifted
yellow food coloring
a selection of writing icings
(available in supermarkets)
ready-made sugar flowers (sold
with the cake ingredients)
paper cake cases

Takes 30 minutes • Makes 20

1 Preheat oven to 375°F. Put the cake cases into bun tins. In a bowl, mix all the cake ingredients and beat with an electric whisk for about 1–2 minutes, until evenly mixed.

2 Put a heaped tablespoon of the cake mixture into the center of each paper case. Bake for 15 minutes, or until golden and well risen. Remove the cakes from the oven and cool on a wire rack.

3 Mix the icing sugar with 4 teaspoons of cold water to make a smooth paste, then color with a drop or two of the yellow food coloring. Spread a teaspoon of the icing on each bun. Leave to set. Using the writing icing, pipe one letter of 'Happy Mother's Day' (or whatever occasion you're celebrating) on to each of the fairy cakes. Leave to set.

• Per fairy cake 186 calories, protein 2g, carbohydrate 28g, fat 8g, saturated fat 5g, fiber trace, added sugar 21g, salt 0.46g

Traditional simnel cake can be a bit too rich – instead, try these light
little muffins with a gooey nugget of marzipan baked in the center.

Simnel Muffins

9oz mixed dried fruit
grated zest and juice of 1 medium
orange
6oz butter, softened
6oz golden caster sugar
3 eggs, beaten
10oz self-raising flour
1 tsp mixed spice
½ tsp freshly grated nutmeg
5 tbsp milk
6oz marzipan

FOR DECORATING
8oz icing sugar
2 tbsp orange juice for mixing
sugar eggs or mini eggs

Takes 55 minutes • Makes 12

1 Tip the fruit into a bowl, add the zest
and juice and microwave on Medium for
2 minutes (or leave to soak for 1 hour). Line
12 deep muffin tins with paper muffin cases.
Preheat oven to 350°F. Beat together the
butter, sugar, eggs, flour, spices and milk until
light and fluffy, about 3–5 minutes. Stir the
fruit in well.
2 Half fill the muffin cases with the mixture.
Divide the marzipan into 12 equal pieces, roll
into balls, then flatten with your thumb. Put
one into each muffin case and spoon the rest
of the mixture over. Bake for 25–30 minutes,
until risen, golden and firm to the touch.
3 Beat together the icing sugar and orange
juice to make icing thick enough to coat the
back of a wooden spoon. Drizzle over the
cooled muffins and top with a cluster of eggs.

• Per muffin 465 calories, protein 6g, carbohydrate
79g, fat 17g, saturated fat 8g, fiber 2g, added sugar
42g, salt 0.61g

This all-in-one cake mixes easily, keeps for a week
wrapped in foil, and freezes well.

Lemon and Violet Drizzle Cake

4oz butter, softened
6oz self-raising flour
1 tsp baking powder
6oz golden caster sugar
2 large eggs
6 tbsp milk
finely grated rind of 1 large lemon

FOR THE ICING AND DECORATION
juice of 1 large lemon (you need
3 tablespoons)
4oz golden caster sugar
crystallized violets and mimosa
balls (or yellow sugar balls), to
decorate

Takes 1 hour • Makes 15

1 Preheat oven to 350°F. Butter and line the base of a shallow oblong tin (about 7 x 11in) with baking paper. Tip all the cake ingredients into a large mixing bowl and beat for 2–3 minutes, until the mixture drops easily off the spoon.

2 Spoon the mixture into the prepared tin and smooth the surface with the back of a spoon. Bake for 30–40 minutes, until golden and firm to the touch. Meanwhile, make the icing: beat together the lemon juice and sugar, pour the mixture evenly over the cake while it is still hot, then leave to cool.

3 Cut the cake into 15 squares. Top each one with a crystallized violet and mimosa ball.

• Per square 175 calories, protein 2g, carbohydrate 29g, fat 7g, saturated fat 4g, fiber none, added sugar 19g, salt 0.3g

These light-as-air cakes are sold in every self-respecting coffee shop in Sydney – try them and you too will be hooked.

Blueberry and Lemon Friands

4oz unsalted butter
4½oz icing sugar, plus extra
for dusting
1oz plain flour
3oz ground almonds
3 egg whites
grated rind of 1 unwaxed lemon 3oz
blueberries

Takes 40 minutes • Serves 6

1 Preheat oven to 400°F. Generously butter six non-stick friand or muffin tins. Melt the butter and set aside to cool.

2 Sift the icing sugar and flour into a bowl. Add the almonds and mix everything between your fingers. Whisk the egg whites in another bowl until they form a light, floppy foam. Make a well in the center of the dry ingredients, tip in the egg whites and lemon rind, then lightly stir in the butter to form a soft batter.

3 Divide the batter among the tins (a large serving spoon is perfect for this job). Sprinkle a handful of blueberries over each cake and bake for 15–20 minutes until just firm to the touch and golden brown. Cool in the tins for 5 minutes, then turn out and cool on a wire rack. To serve, dust lightly with icing sugar.

• Per friand 316 calories, protein 5g, carbohydrate 27g, fat 22g, saturated fat 9g, fiber 1g, added sugar 22g, salt 0.09g

These little cakes are easy – fun to make
and decorate with the kids.

Blackberry Fairy Cakes

5fl oz carton low-fat natural yogurt
(rinse the pot and use
as a measure)
1 pot of caster sugar
1 pot of sunflower oil
2 eggs
2 pots of self-raising flour
9oz punnet blackberries, plus
extra for decorating
finely grated rind of 1 orange

FOR THE ICING AND DECORATION
1 pot of icing sugar, plus extra
for dusting
1 tbsp orange juice
orange food coloring (optional)
2oz bar dark chocolate, melted

Takes 35 minutes • Makes 18

1 Preheat oven to 375°F. Line two bun tins with 18 paper cases. Tip the yogurt, sugar, oil and eggs into a bowl and whisk until combined. Tip in the flour, three quarters of the blackberries and half the orange rind; fold into the mixture with a large metal spoon – don't overwork.

2 Fill each bun case three-quarters full with the mixture and bake for 20–25 minutes until the cakes are risen and golden. Turn out and cool on a wire rack.

3 Sift the icing sugar into a bowl, add the remaining orange rind and the orange juice to make a smooth icing. Stir in a few drops of orange food coloring, if you like. Using a teaspoon, spoon a little icing on top of each cooled cake. Decorate with extra blackberries, or drizzled melted chocolate.

• Per fairy cake 177 calories, protein 3g, carbohydrate 29g, fat 7g, saturated fat 2g, fiber 1g, added sugar 18g, salt 0.15g

Ideal with a cup of tea at home, or to enjoy
at your next picnic.

Apricot Crumb Squares

FOR THE TOPPING
6oz plain flour
5oz light muscovado sugar
5oz butter, softened
1 tsp ground cinnamon
½ tsp salt

FOR THE CAKE
6oz butter, softened
8oz golden caster sugar
3 large eggs
6oz plain flour
1 tsp baking powder
2–3 tbsp milk
8 fresh apricots (or canned in
natural juice), quartered
icing sugar, for dusting

Takes 1¼ hours • Makes 16

1 Preheat oven to 350ºF, and butter a shallow 9in square cake tin. Put the five topping ingredients in a food processor and blend to make a sticky crumble.
2 In a separate bowl, blend the butter, sugar, eggs, flour and baking powder using an electric hand whisk or wooden spoon, gradually adding enough milk to make a creamy mixture that drops from a spoon. Spread in the tin and scatter with apricots. Top with the crumble and press down.
3 Bake for 45–50 minutes until golden and a skewer inserted comes out clean. Cool in the tin, cut into 16 squares and dust with icing sugar.

• Per square 332 calories, protein 4g, carbohydrate 42g, fat 18g, saturated fat 11g, fiber 1g, added sugar 22g, salt 0.52g

These moist but crumbly squares are best eaten on the day,
but will freeze for up to 3 months.

Blackcurrant Crumble Squares

4oz butter, softened
6oz caster sugar
1 egg
10oz self-raising flour
½ cup milk
8oz fresh blackcurrants,
destalked

FOR THE CRUMBLE
4oz caster sugar
3oz plain flour
finely grated rind of 1 lemon
2oz butter

Takes 1 hour • Makes 12

1 Preheat oven to 350°F. Butter a
12 x 7in oblong cake tin and line with baking
paper. (You could also use a 9in square tin or
a 10in round tin.)
2 Beat the butter and sugar in a large bowl
with an electric hand whisk until the mixture is
pale and fluffy. Whisk in the egg, then carefully
fold in the flour and milk until thoroughly
combined. Spoon into the tin and spread
evenly. Sprinkle over the blackcurrants.
3 Mix together the sugar, flour and lemon
rind. Rub in the butter until the mixture is
crumbly, then sprinkle on top of the squares.
Bake for 45 minutes until the topping is
golden and the blackcurrants start to burst
through; leave to cool in the tin. When cool,
lift the cake out, and cut into squares.

• Per square 315 calories, protein 4g, carbohydrate
50g, fat 13g, saturated fat 8g, fiber 2g, added sugar
25g, salt 0.29g

Light and chocolatey, these are the perfect
Halloween treat.

Spider Web Chocolate Fudge Muffins

2oz dark chocolate, broken
into pieces
3oz butter
1 tbsp milk
8oz self-raising flour
½ tsp bicarbonate of soda
3oz light muscovado sugar
2oz golden caster sugar
1 egg
4fl oz carton sour cream

FOR THE TOPPING
4oz dark chocolate, broken
into pieces and melted
4oz white chocolate, broken
into pieces and melted

Takes 50 minutes • Makes 10

1 Preheat oven to 375ºF, and line a muffin tin
with 10 paper cases. Heat the chocolate and
butter with the milk until melted. Stir and cool.
2 Mix the flour, bicarbonate of soda and both
sugars. Beat the egg in another bowl and stir
in the sour cream, then pour this on the flour
mixture and add the cooled chocolate. Stir
just to combine – don't overmix. Spoon into
the cases to about three-quarters full. Bake
for 20 minutes until well risen. Cool in the tins
for a few minutes, then lift out and continue
to cool on a wire rack.
3 Spread one muffin with dark chocolate,
then pipe four circles of white chocolate on
top. Drag a skewer from center to the edge
to create a cobweb effect. Alternate dark
chocolate on white for the opposite effect.

• Per mufffin 349 calories, protein 5g, carbohydrate
45g, fat 18g, saturated fat 9g, fiber 1g, added sugar
28g, salt 0.59g

Top with marzipan stars or meringue before baking
to vary this festive recipe.

Festive Mince Pies

FOR THE PASTRY
8oz plain flour
2oz ground almonds
5oz butter, chopped into small pieces
grated rind of 1 orange
2oz caster sugar
1 egg yolk

FOR THE FILLING AND DECORATION
8oz mincemeat
1 egg white, lightly whisked
caster sugar, for dusting

Takes 40 minutes, plus 30 minutes chilling time • Makes 18

1 Preheat oven to 400°F. Whiz the flour, almonds, butter, orange rind and sugar into crumbs. Add the egg yolk and a teaspoon of cold water and pulse until it forms a dough. Wrap in plastic wrap and chill for 30 minutes.

2 Roll out the dough thinly and stamp out eighteen 3in rounds. Use to line bun tins. Put a heaped teaspoon of mincemeat in each pastry case. Stamp out nine more pastry rounds. Cut out festive shapes from the centre of each round.

3 Cover the pies with the shapes and pastry rounds with the centers removed. Brush the tops with egg white and dust lightly with caster sugar. Bake for 12–15 minutes until the pastry is crisp and golden. Cool in the tins for 5 minutes, then cool on a wire rack.

• Per mince pie 164 calories, protein 2g, carbohydrate 20g, fat 9g, saturated fat 5g, fiber 1g, added sugar 9g, salt 0.17g

Absolutely delicious with a cup of tea,
these bars are also dairy-free.

Sticky Apricot and Almond Bars

4oz whole blanched almonds
9oz ready-to-eat dried apricots
3oz porridge oats
3oz plain flour
1 tsp baking powder
9fl oz jar apple sauce
2 tbsp sunflower oil
1 egg, beaten
2 tbsp apricot jam or conserve

Takes 55 minutes • Makes 15

1 Preheat oven to 350°F. Oil and line the base of an 7in square tin. Roughly chop the almonds into fairly large chunks to give a good texture and finely chop the apricots to give a stickiness to the bars.

2 Put all the dry ingredients in a large bowl. Combine the apple sauce, oil and egg, and add to the dry ingredients. Mix until everything is combined and gooey. Spoon the mixture into the prepared tin, level the surface and bake for 40 minutes or until firm and springy to the touch.

3 Allow to cool in the tin for a couple of minutes, then loosen the sides and turn out on to a wire rack. Warm the apricot jam for 2–3 minutes. Then brush over the surface of the cooled bars, cut into 15 slices and enjoy.

• Per bar 145 calories, protein 4g, carbohydrate 19g, fat 6g, saturated fat 1g, fiber 2g, added sugar 3g, salt 0.13g

Margaret Fineran, who created this recipe, was a chef
at the American Embassy in London.

Margaret's Caramel Nut Squares

FOR THE PASTRY
6oz plain flour
2oz icing sugar
3oz cold butter, cut into cubes
¼ tsp vanilla extract
1 small egg, beaten

FOR THE FILLING
3oz granulated sugar
6oz clear honey
2oz butter
1½ cup heavy cream
4oz pecan nuts, toasted
4oz flaked almonds, toasted
4oz whole hazelnuts, toasted
4oz pistachios, unsalted,
toasted
2oz dried cranberries
whipped cream, to serve

Takes 1¼ hours, plus 4 hours
freezing • Makes 9

1 Preheat oven to 350°F. Whiz together the flour, icing sugar and butter. Add the vanilla and beaten egg and pulse until the pastry comes together. Chill, wrapped in plastic wrap, for 30 minutes.

2 Roll the pastry out on a lightly floured surface and use to line a 9in square tin. Pre-bake for 7 minutes. Bring the sugar and honey to a boil without stirring. In a separate pan, heat the butter with the cream until hot. When the sugar mixture is boiling, pour in the hot cream and butter, and simmer, stirring, for 2–3 minutes.

3 Mix in the nuts and cranberries. Spoon into the hot pastry case. Return to the oven for 7 minutes. Remove, cool, then cover and freeze for 3–4 hours. Cut into squares, thaw for 30 minutes, and serve with the cream.

• Per square 743 calories, protein 10g, carbohydrate 54g, fat 55g, saturated fat 19g, fiber 3g, added sugar 31g, salt 0.35g

The solution for any picnic or open-air event – packed with good things, and easy to make.

Sunshine Bars

4oz dried ready-to-eat tropical medley or other mixed dried fruits
4oz porridge oats
2oz puffed rice cereal, such as Rice Krispies
3oz desiccated coconut
2oz blanched hazelnuts or shelled peanuts or other nuts
2oz sunflower, sesame or pumpkin seeds
4oz light muscovado sugar
½ cup golden syrup
4oz butter, cut into pieces

Takes 25 minutes, plus 2 hours setting time • Makes 18

1 Chop the tropical medley into pieces using kitchen scissors. Tip the oats, cereal, coconut and fruit into a large bowl and mix well. Put the hazelnuts and sunflower, sesame or pumpkin seeds in a large frying pan with no oil and, over a moderate heat, stir until they are lightly toasted. Leave to cool a little then tip into the bowl and mix.

2 Put the sugar, syrup and butter in a small pan and heat gently, stirring with a wooden spoon until melted, then simmer for 2 minutes until slightly thicker and syrupy. Quickly stir the syrup into the dry ingredients, mixing until well blended with no dry patches.

3 Quickly tip into a 8in square tin and press down with the back of a spoon to even out the surface. Leave to cool and set – about 2 hours. Cut the mixture into 18 bars.

• Per bar 190 calories, protein 2g, carbohydrate 22g, fat 11g, saturated fat 6g, fiber 2g, added sugar 11g, salt 0.26g

By using different-sized tins and varying the cooking time,
this recipe can be adapted to suit all tastes.

Classic Oatmeal Squares

6oz butter, cut into pieces
5oz golden syrup
2oz light muscovado sugar
9oz oats

Takes 35 minutes • Makes 12

1 Preheat oven to 350°F. Line the base of a shallow 9in square tin with a sheet of baking paper if the tin is not non-stick. (Use a 8in square tin for a thicker, chewier flapjack). Put the butter, syrup and sugar in a medium pan. Stir over a low heat until the butter has melted and the sugar has dissolved. Remove from the heat and stir in the oats.

2 Press the mixture into the tin. Bake for 20–25 minutes, until golden brown on top (follow the longer cooking time for a crispier flapjack). Allow to cool in the tin for 5 minutes then mark into bars or squares with the back of a knife while still warm. Cool in the tin completely before cutting and removing – this prevents the squares from breaking up.

• Per square 242 calories, protein 3g, carbohydrate 29g, fat 14g, saturated fat 8g, fiber 1g, added sugar 13g, salt 0.38g

This easy-mix bar is the perfect bake – all you do is weigh, mix and scatter everything into the tin.

Raspberry and Pine Nut Bars

8oz plain flour
8oz porridge oats
9oz pack butter, cut into small pieces and softened
6oz light muscovado sugar
finely grated zest of 1 lemon
4oz pack pine nuts
9oz raspberries

Takes 1 hour • Makes 12

1 Preheat oven to 375°F. Butter a shallow 9in square tin. Tip the flour, oats and butter into a mixing bowl and work together with your fingers to make coarse crumbs. Mix in the sugar, lemon zest and three quarters of the pine nuts using your hands, then press the mixture together well so it forms large sticky clumps.

2 Drop about two thirds of the oat mixture into the tin, spread it out and press down very lightly – don't pack it too firmly. Scatter the raspberries on top, sprinkle the rest of the oat mixture over, then the rest of the pine nuts and press everything down lightly.

3 Bake for 35–40 minutes until pale golden on top. Cut into 12 bars with a sharp knife while still warm, then leave to cool in the tin before removing.

• Per bar 391 calories, protein 6g, carbohydrate 40g, fat 24g, saturated fat 12g, fiber 3g, added sugar 15g, salt 0.41g

These cakes are truly scrumptious and
so simple to whip together.

Starry Toffee Cake Squares

8oz butter
8oz golden syrup
10oz self-raising flour
1 tsp salt
8oz light muscovado sugar
3 eggs
2 tbsp milk
8oz yellow marzipan
red and green food coloring
icing sugar, for dusting

Takes 1½ hours • Makes 24

1 Preheat oven to 325°F. Butter and line the base of a 13 x 9 x 1in Swiss roll tin. Gently melt the butter and syrup in a pan, stirring to combine. Cool for 15 minutes.
2 Sift the flour with the salt and stir in the muscovado sugar. Beat in the cooled syrup mixture. Beat the eggs and milk, and combine with the flour mixture until smooth. Pour into the tin and level with a spoon. Bake for 40–50 minutes until risen and firm in the center. Leave in the tin to cool for 10 minutes. Tip on to a wire rack until cold.
3 Divide the marzipan into three; color one piece with red and another with green coloring. Roll out and cut out star shapes. Cut the cake into 24 squares, top with marzipan stars and dust with icing sugar.

• Per square 217 calories, protein 3g, carbohydrate 34g, fat 9g, saturated fat 5g, fiber 1g, added sugar 22g, salt 0.37g

This is one of those great treats that you can just
sling together and bake.

Golden Orange and Walnut Squares

9oz unsalted butter, chopped
into pieces
9oz golden caster sugar
6oz golden syrup
15oz porridge oats
2oz walnut pieces
finely grated zest of 1 large orange
3 tbsp fine-cut orange marmalade

Takes 55 minutes • Makes 12

1 Preheat oven to 350°F, and generously
butter a 12 x 7in shallow baking tin. Melt the
butter, sugar and syrup over a medium heat,
stirring constantly. Take off the heat and stir
in the oats, walnuts and orange zest. The
mixture should be quite soft.
2 Tip the mixture into the tin and level it off.
Bake for around 30 minutes, until the edges
are golden brown but the center is still a little
soft. Remove from the oven and mark into
12 pieces while it is still warm, cutting
halfway through with a knife. Leave to cool.
3 Heat the marmalade with 1 tbsp water
until it becomes syrupy. Brush this glaze over
the squares mixture and leave to cool before
cutting into 12 pieces. They will keep in an
airtight tin for up to a week.

• Per square 455 calories, protein 7g, carbohydrate
60g, fat 22g, saturated fat 12g, fiber 4g, added sugar
36g, salt 0.12g

Combining fruit with fiber is a great energy boost.

Bramley Apple, Fig and Walnut Squares

1lb Bramley apples, peeled and cored
1oz golden caster sugar
grated zest of 1 small lemon
4oz dried ready-to-eat figs, roughly chopped
5oz butter, cut in pieces
2oz light muscovado sugar
5oz golden syrup
9oz porridge oats
½ tsp ground cinnamon
1oz walnuts, finely chopped

Takes 1¼ hours • Makes 9

1 Preheat oven to 375°F. Slice the apples into a small saucepan and stir in the caster sugar. Bring to a boil, cover and simmer for 10 minutes or until the apple is soft, stirring occasionally. Stir in the zest and figs and cook for a further 15 minutes, uncovered, stirring often until the figs are softened and the mixture is quite dry. Whiz to a purée in a food processor.

2 Melt the butter, muscovado sugar and syrup in a saucepan, but don't let it boil. Stir in the oats and cinnamon and mix well.

3 Press half the mixture into an 7in shallow square sandwich tin. Spread the purée on top and cover with the remaining mixture. Sprinkle over the walnut pieces and bake for 25 minutes or until golden. Remove from the oven, mark into squares and cool.

• Per square 516 calories, protein 6g, carbohydrate 66g, fat 27g, saturated fat 14g, fiber 5g, added sugar 24g, salt 0.61g

These are chewier than most oat bars because of the bananas mashed throughout.

Chewy Gooey Squares

5oz butter
4oz light muscovado sugar
2 heaped tbsp golden syrup
12oz porridge oats (not jumbo oats)
1 tsp ground cinnamon
½ tsp baking powder
2 medium, ripe bananas

Takes 45 minutes • Makes 18

1 Preheat oven to 350°F. Butter a 9 x 13in Swiss roll tin. Melt together the butter, sugar and syrup in a large saucepan over a low heat, then stir in the oats, cinnamon, baking powder and a pinch of salt until well combined. Peel and mash the bananas and add to the mixture, stirring well to combine. Tip into the prepared tin and smooth the surface with the back of a metal spoon.

2 Bake for 20–25 minutes or until the edges are just beginning to turn golden brown. The mixture will feel fairly firm to the touch.

3 Transfer the tin to a wire rack and cut the mixture into bars while still hot. Leave until completely cold before removing with a palette knife.

• Per square 176 calories, protein 3g, carbohydrate 25g, fat 8g, saturated fat 4g, fiber 1g, added sugar 8g, salt 0.23g

This bar is deservedly a *Good Food* favorite.

Apple and Apricot Treacle Tart Bars

FOR THE SHORTBREAD BASE
4oz butter, softened
2oz light muscovado sugar
6oz plain flour

FOR THE FRUIT FILLING
1lb (about 2 medium) cooking
apples, cored, peeled and
chopped
1oz caster sugar
6oz ready-to-eat dried
apricots, halved

FOR THE TREACLE TART TOPPING
grated rind of 1 orange, plus
1 tbsp juice
8oz golden syrup
8 tbsp porridge oats

Takes 1½ hours • Makes 12

1 Preheat oven to 325°F. Beat the butter and sugar until fluffy. Stir in the flour until smooth. Tip the mixture into a 9in square tin and press down on the base. Lightly prick with a fork and bake for 15 minutes. Set aside to cool.
2 Put the apples in a pan with the sugar. Cover loosely and cook over a low heat, stirring occasionally, for about 10 minutes or until the apples are pulpy. Add the apricots and cook gently, uncovered, for a further 15 minutes, stirring. Whiz to a purée.
3 Increase the oven heat to 375°F. Spread the filling over the base. Combine the topping ingredients until well mixed. Spread over the filling. Return to the oven for a further 20–30 minutes, until set and pale golden. Cool in the tin before cutting.

• Per bar 251 calories, protein 3g, carbohydrate 45g, fat 8g, saturated fat 5g, fiber 3g, added sugar 20g, salt 0.29g

Containing marmalade, granola, orange juice and dried apricots, these muffins make a wonderful start to your day.

Breakfast Munching Muffins

4oz ready-to-eat dried
apricots, chopped
4 tbsp orange juice
2 large eggs
4oz carton sour cream
3½fl oz sunflower oil
3oz golden caster sugar
10oz self-raising flour, sifted
1 tsp baking powder
2oz crunchy granola
12 heaped tsp marmalade

FOR THE TOPPING
2oz light muscovado sugar
2 tbsp sunflower oil
2oz crunchy granola

Takes 1 hour, plus 20 minutes
soaking • Makes 12

1 Preheat oven to 375°F. Soak the apricots in the orange juice for 20 minutes or so to plump them up.
2 Beat the eggs in a medium bowl, then mix in the sour cream, oil and sugar. Stir into the apricot mixture. Put the flour, baking powder and granola in a large bowl, then gently stir in the apricot mixture. Combine thoroughly but quickly – don't overmix or the muffins will be tough.
3 Spoon the mixture into 12 muffin cases (the large paper cases) in a muffin tray. Dip your thumb into a little flour, then make a fairly deep thumbprint in each muffin. Fill each with a heaped teaspoon of marmalade.
4 Combine the topping ingredients and sprinkle over the top of the muffins. Bake for 25–30 minutes, until well risen and golden.

• Per muffin 322 calories, protein 5g, carbohydrate 48g, fat 14g, saturated fat 3g, fiber 2g, added sugar 19g, salt 0.51g

These deliciously moist muffins use soy flour, and also contain whole wheat flour and sunflower oil to keep them 'heart friendly'.

Banana and Walnut Muffins

4oz whole wheat flour
1oz soya flour
3 tbsp caster sugar
2 tsp baking powder
3oz walnuts, roughly chopped
1 egg, beaten
½ cup sweetened soy milk
½ cup sunflower oil
2 large bananas, about 8oz when peeled, roughly chopped

FOR THE DECORATION
3 tbsp apricot jam
2oz chopped walnuts

Takes 40 minutes • Makes 6

1 Preheat oven to 400°F. Line six muffin tins with paper muffin cases or oil the tins. Mix together the first five ingredients in a bowl with a pinch of salt and make a well in the center.

2 In another bowl, mix together the egg, soy milk and oil. Pour this mixture into the flour and stir until just blended. Gently stir in the bananas. Spoon the mixture into the muffin cases, filling them to about two-thirds full. Bake for 25–30 minutes, until a skewer inserted comes out clean. Transfer the muffins to a wire rack.

3 Gently heat the jam and brush it on top of the muffins. Sprinkle over the walnuts and serve warm.

• Per muffin 425 calories, protein 9g, carbohydrate 41g, fat 26g, saturated fat 3g, fiber 3g, added sugar 17g, salt 0.89g

These low-fat muffins are great to grab when you don't
have time to sit down to breakfast.

Fruitburst Muffins

8oz plain flour
2 tsp baking powder
2 large eggs
2oz butter, melted
3¼ cup skimmed milk
3½fl oz clear honey
5oz fresh blueberries
3oz dried cranberries
5oz seedless raisins
5oz dried apricots, chopped
1 tsp grated orange zest
1 tsp ground cinnamon

Takes 50 minutes • Makes 12

1 Preheat oven to 400°F, and very lightly butter a 12-hole muffin tin. Sift the flour and baking powder into a bowl. In another bowl, lightly beat the eggs, then stir in the melted butter, milk and honey.

2 Add the egg mixture to the flour mixture with the remaining ingredients. Combine quickly without overworking (it's fine if there are some lumps left – you want it gloopy rather than fluid). Spoon the mixture into the muffin tin. Bake for 20–25 minutes until well risen and pale golden on top.

3 Leave in the tin for a few minutes before turning out. When cool, they'll keep in an airtight tin for two days. They can also be frozen for up to one month.

• Per muffin 243 calories, protein 5g, carbohydrate 41g, fat 8g, saturated fat 3g, fiber 2g, added sugar 6g, salt 0.59g

Other seasonal berries such as raspberries, loganberries and blueberries also add a delicious fruitiness to these muffins.

Blackberry Muffins

14oz plain flour
6oz caster sugar
1 tbsp baking powder
finely grated zest of 1 orange
½ tsp salt
1¼ cup carton buttermilk
2 eggs, beaten
3oz butter, melted
9oz blackberries

Takes 30 minutes • Makes 12

1 Preheat oven to 400ºF. Butter a 12-hole muffin tin. In a large bowl, combine the flour, sugar, baking powder, zest and salt. In a separate bowl, mix together the buttermilk, eggs and butter.

2 Make a well in the center of the dry ingredients and pour in the buttermilk mixture. Stir until the ingredients are just combined and the mixture is quite stiff, but be careful not to overmix. Lightly fold in the blackberries, then spoon the mixture into the tins to fill the holes generously.

3 Bake for 15–18 minutes until risen and pale golden on top. Leave to cool in the tin for a few minutes, as the muffins are quite delicate when hot. Run a palette knife around the edge of the muffins and carefully transfer to a wire rack to cool. Best eaten the same day.

• Per muffin 252 calories, protein 5g, carbohydrate 44g, fat 7g, saturated fat 4g, fiber 2g, added sugar 15g, salt 0.79g

Each muffin hides a surprise filling of fresh fruit
and creamy cheese.

Strawberry Cheesecake Muffins

12oz plain flour
1½ tbsp baking powder
5oz caster sugar
finely grated rind of 2 medium
oranges
½ tsp salt
2 eggs
9fl oz milk
3oz butter, melted

FOR THE FILLING
6oz half-fat cream cheese
3 tbsp caster sugar
6 small strawberries, halved

Takes 40 minutes • Makes 12

1 Preheat oven to 400°F. Line a muffin tin with 12 paper cases. Sift the flour and baking powder into a large bowl, then stir in the sugar, orange rind and salt. Beat the eggs and milk together in a jug or bowl, then stir in the butter and gently mix into the dry ingredients to make a loose, slightly lumpy mixture. Do not overmix or the muffins will be tough.

2 Mix together the cream cheese and sugar for the filling. Half-fill the paper cases with the muffin mixture, then push half a strawberry into each. Top with a teaspoon of sweet cheese, then spoon over the remaining muffin mixture to cover and fill the muffin cases.

3 Bake for 15 minutes until well risen and golden on top. Remove from the tin and allow to cool completely on a wire rack.

• Per muffin 293 calories, protein 6g, carbohydrate 42g, fat 12g, saturated fat 5g, fiber 1g, added sugar 18g, salt 1.03g

Banana chips add extra flavor and a crunchy
texture to these muffins.

Banana and Lemon Muffins

3oz honey-dipped dried
banana chips
5oz self-raising flour
2 tsp baking powder
finely grated zest and juice of
1 lemon
4 tbsp light muscovado sugar
5 tbsp milk
1 egg, beaten
½cup sunflower oil
3 bananas
4 tbsp icing sugar

Takes 45 minutes • Makes 7

1 Preheat oven to 400°F. Lightly oil seven
cups of a muffin tin or line with deep paper
cases. Break 2oz of the banana chips into
pieces. Sift together the flour and baking
powder. Stir in the zest, sugar and the broken
dried banana chips.

2 Whisk together the milk, egg and oil. Mash
the bananas with 1 tablespoon of lemon juice.
Fold carefully into the dry ingredients with the
egg mixture (do not overwork it). Divide the
mixture between the muffin cups/cases, not
quite filling them. Bake for 20 minutes until
risen and firm. Leave for a few minutes, then
transfer to a wire rack to cool.

3 Sift the icing sugar into a bowl. Blend
with 1–2 teaspoons of the remaining lemon
juice. Drizzle over the muffins; decorate with
the remaining whole banana chips.

• Per muffin 332 calories, protein 4g, carbohydrate
57g, fat 11g, saturated fat 1g, fiber 1g, added sugar
25g, salt 0.76g

If you like the taste of banana loaf, you'll love these moist muffins.

Banana Pecan Muffins

9oz plain flour
1oz natural wheatgerm
1 tsp bicarbonate of soda
1 tsp baking powder
½ tsp ground cinnamon
4oz pecans, roughly chopped
3 small bananas (12oz total
weight in their skins)
1 egg, beaten
3oz butter, melted
4oz light muscovado sugar
6fl oz buttermilk

Takes 40 minutes • Makes 8

1 Preheat oven to 400ºF. Butter 8 holes of a muffin tin. In a large bowl, combine the flour, wheatgerm, bicarbonate, baking powder, cinnamon and 3oz pecans. Peel and mash the bananas.

2 In a separate bowl, mix together the egg, butter and sugar, then stir in the mashed banana and buttermilk. Add the egg mixture all at once to the flour mixture, stirring until just combined, but don't overmix or the result will be heavy.

3 Spoon the mixture into the holes to fill. Sprinkle with the remaining pecans. Bake for 20–25 minutes until well risen and golden. Leave in the tin for 10 minutes, then remove and cool on a wire rack.

• Per muffin 376 calories, protein 7g, carbohydrate 47g, fat 19g, saturated fat 6g, fiber 2g, added sugar 13g, salt 0.89g

This mixture will also divide between a 12-hole muffin tin for smaller muffins.

Squash, Cinnamon and Pumpkin Seed Muffins

10oz plain flour
1 tbsp baking powder
2 tsp ground cinnamon
1 tsp salt
3 eggs
3¼ cup milk
3oz butter, melted
6oz light muscovado sugar
12oz peeled, grated butternut squash
small handful of green pumpkin seeds

Takes 50 minutes • Makes 9

1 Preheat oven to 400ºF. Lightly butter a 9-hole muffin tin or line with paper muffin cases. Sift together the flour, baking powder, cinnamon and salt and put aside.

2 In a large bowl, mix the eggs, milk and butter. Add the sugar and beat well. Add the flour mixture and beat to give a lumpy batter. Stir in the grated squash.

3 Fill the nine holes of the muffin tin (or paper cases) to the top with the mixture, sprinkle the pumpkin seeds on top. Bake for 20–25 minutes until well risen and firm to the touch. Cool slightly in the tin, turn out and cool on a wire rack.

• Per muffin 317 calories, protein 7g, carbohydrate 50g, fat 12g, saturated fat 6g, fiber 2g, added sugar 20g, salt 1.52g

These muffins have the bonus of lots of health-giving ingredients – so enjoy them without guilt!

Feel-good Muffins

6oz self-raising flour
2oz porridge oats
5oz light muscovado sugar
2 tsp ground cinnamon
½ tsp bicarbonate of soda
1 egg, beaten
½ cup buttermilk
1 tsp vanilla extract
6 tbsp sunflower oil
6oz pitted prunes, chopped
3oz pecans

Takes 45 minutes • Makes 6–8

1 Preheat oven to 400°F. Butter 6–8 muffin tins or line them with muffin cases. Put the flour, oats, sugar, cinnamon and bicarbonate of soda in a large bowl, then rub everything through your fingers, as if making pastry, to ensure the ingredients are evenly blended.
2 In a separate bowl, beat the egg, then stir in the buttermilk, vanilla and oil. Lightly stir the egg mixture into the flour. Fold in the prunes and nuts.
3 Divide between the tins, filling the cases to the brim, then bake for 20–25 minutes until risen and golden. Serve warm or cold.

• Per muffin (for six) 478 calories, protein 8g, carbohydrate 66g, fat 22g, saturated fat 2g, fiber 2g, added sugar 24g, salt 0.66g

Although best made with fresh blueberries, you can make these muffins using the same amount of frozen berries.

Berry Buttermilk Muffins

14oz plain flour
6oz caster sugar
1 tbsp baking powder
finely grated rind of 1 lemon
½ tsp salt
1¼ cup carton buttermilk
2 eggs, beaten
3oz butter, melted
9oz fresh or frozen blueberries, or mixed summer fruits, used straight from frozen

Takes 40 minutes • Makes 12

1 Preheat oven to 400°F. Butter a 12-hole muffin tin. In a large bowl, combine the flour, sugar, baking powder, lemon rind and salt. In a separate bowl, mix together the buttermilk, eggs and butter.

2 Make a well in the center of the dry ingredients and pour in the buttermilk mixture. Stir until the ingredients are just combined and the mixture is quite stiff, but don't overmix. Lightly fold in the berries, then spoon the mixture into the tins to fill generously.

3 Bake for about 25 minutes until risen and pale golden on top. Leave to cool in the tin for about 5 minutes before turning out on to a wire rack, as the muffins are quite delicate when hot.

• Per muffin 253 calories, protein 5g, carbohydrate 44g, fat 7g, saturated fat 4g, fiber 1g, added sugar 15g, salt 0.91g

A fluffy light muffin, ideal for lunch alongside big chunks of cheese, or as a snack spread with butter and drizzled with extra honey.

Oat and Honey Muffins

9oz plain flour
3oz porridge oats
1 tbsp baking powder
½ tsp cinnamon
½ tsp salt
3oz raisins
2 eggs, beaten
7fl oz milk
2½fl oz vegetable oil
2oz light muscovado sugar
5 tbsp clear honey

Takes 40 minutes • Makes 8

1 Preheat oven to 400°F. Butter 8 holes of a muffin tin. In a large bowl, combine the flour, oats, baking powder, cinnamon, salt and raisins. In a separate bowl, mix together the eggs, milk, oil, sugar and honey. Stir this into the flour mixture until just combined, but don't overmix – the mixture should be quite runny.
2 Spoon the mixture into the holes to fill. Bake for 20–25 minutes. Leave in the tin for a few minutes. Leave in the tin for a few minutes, then turn out on to a wire rack to cool.

• Per muffin 349 calories, protein 7g, carbohydrate 57g, fat 12g, saturated fat 2g, fiber 2g, added sugar 16g, salt 1.18g

Serve these muffins warm, drizzled with a generous
helping of maple syrup.

Cranberry and Poppy Seed Muffins

4oz unsalted butter
10fl oz carton sour cream
2 large free-range eggs
1 tsp vanilla extract
10oz plain flour
2 tsp baking powder
1 tsp baking soda
½ tsp salt
8oz golden caster sugar
4 tsp poppy seeds
5oz fresh or frozen cranberries (thawed)
maple syrup, to serve

Takes 50 minutes • Makes 10

1 Preheat oven to 375°F. Line 10 muffin tins with large discs of very loosely scrunched and lightly oiled greaseproof paper (they should come up the sides of the tin so they become paper muffin cases). Melt the butter, leave to cool for a minute or two, then beat in the sour cream, followed by the eggs and the vanilla extract.

2 In another bowl, mix the flour, baking powder, bicarbonate of soda, salt, sugar and poppy seeds together. Stir this into the sour cream mixture along with the cranberries.

3 Fill each of the prepared muffin cases generously with the mixture and bake for 20–25 minutes. Test with a skewer – it should pull out clean if muffins are done. Lift on to a cooling rack, spoon over some maple syrup and eat while they are still warm.

• Per muffin 340 calories, protein 6g, carbohydrate 45g, fat 16g, saturated fat 9g, fiber 1g, added sugar 21g, salt 0.98g

No chance of keeping these for more than a day – definitely a muffin to eat while still warm and the chocolate is gooey.

Triple Chocolate Chunk Muffins

9oz plain flour
1oz cocoa powder
2 tsp baking powder
½ tsp baking soda
3oz each dark and white chocolate, broken into chunks
4oz milk chocolate, broken into chunks
2 eggs, beaten
10fl oz carton sour cream
3oz light muscovado sugar
3oz butter, melted

Takes 35 minutes • Makes 11

1 Preheat oven to 400°F. Butter 11 holes of a muffin tin. In a large bowl, combine the flour, cocoa, baking powder, bicarbonate of soda and chocolate. In a separate bowl, mix together the eggs, soured cream, sugar and butter.
2 Add the sour cream mixture to the flour mixture and stir until just combined and the mixture is fairly stiff, but don't overmix. Spoon the mixture into the holes to generously fill.
3 Bake for 20 minutes until well risen. Leave in the tins for about 15 minutes as the mixture is quite tender. Remove from the tins and cool on a wire rack.

• Per muffin 325 calories, protein 6g, carbohydrate 37g, fat 18g, saturated fat 11g, fiber 1g, added sugar 17g, salt 0.72g

There are no clever techniques involved with Angela Nilsen's irresistible cookies – just measure, mix, stir and bake.

Angela's All-American Chocolate Chunk Cookies

11oz dark chocolate (about 55% cocoa solids), broken into small chunks
4oz bar milk chocolate, broken into small chunks
4oz light muscovado sugar
3oz butter, softened
4oz crunchy peanut butter
1 medium egg
½ tsp vanilla extract
4oz self-raising flour
4oz large salted roasted peanuts

Takes 50 minutes • Makes 12

1 Preheat oven to 350°F. Melt 4oz of the dark chocolate chunks. Stir, then tip in the sugar, butter, peanut butter, egg and vanilla and beat with a wooden spoon until well mixed. Stir in the flour, all the milk chocolate chunks, the nuts and half the remaining dark chocolate chunks. The mixture will feel quite soft.

2 Drop big spoonfuls in 12 piles on to 2 or 3 baking sheets, leaving room for them to spread. Stick 2–3 pieces of the remaining dark chocolate chunks into each cookie.

3 Bake for 10–12 minutes until they are tinged slightly darker around the edges. They will be soft in the middle, but will crisp up as they cool. Cook for longer and you'll have crisper cookies. Leave to cool for a few minutes, then transfer to a wire rack.

• Per cookie 381 calories, protein 7g, carbohydrate 36g, fat 24g, saturated fat 10g, fiber 2g, added sugar 27g, salt 0.42g

Creamed coconut adds richness and flavor
to these cookies.

Coconut and Cashew Cookies

5oz unsalted cashews, toasted
3oz creamed coconut, grated
6oz plain flour
½ tsp baking powder
5oz butter, softened
4½oz dark muscovado sugar
1 tbsp ground ginger
1 egg

Takes 35 minutes • Makes 14–16

1 Preheat oven to 350°F. Split some cashews in half; leave the rest whole. Mix with the coconut and set aside.
2 Blend the remaining ingredients in a food processor to make a smooth, stiff consistency. Set aside four tablespoonfuls of the nut mixture; stir the rest into the flour mixture.
3 Put 14–16 heaped tablespoons of the mixture in mounds, well apart, on buttered baking sheets. Flatten slightly with your fingers. Sprinkle with the reserved nut mixture and bake for 10–12 minutes until golden and set at the edges. Leave for a few minutes, then cool on a rack. The cookies will stay fresh for up to 1 week in an airtight container.

• Per cookie (for fourteen) 262 calories, protein 4g, carbohydrate 22g, fat 18g, saturated fat 9g, fiber 2g, added sugar 9g, salt 0.34g

Make these treats for your next birthday party –
for kids or adults.

Smarties Cookies

4oz butter, softened
4oz light muscovado sugar
1 tbsp golden syrup
6oz self-raising flour
3oz Smarties (about 3 tubes)

Takes 20 minutes • Makes 14

1 Preheat oven to 350°F. Beat the butter and sugar in a bowl until light and creamy, then beat in the syrup.
2 Work in half the flour. Stir in the Smarties with the remaining flour and work the dough together with your fingers. Divide into 14 balls. Place them well apart on baking sheets. Do not flatten them.
3 Bake for 12 minutes until pale golden at the edges. Cool on a wire rack. These cookies will keep for up to 4 days in an airtight tin.

• Per cookie 167 calories, protein 2g, carbohydrate 23g, fat 8g, saturated fat 5g, fiber trace, added sugar 13g, salt 0.3g

Store any uncooked mixture in the fridge for up to 1 week, or freeze on the day for up to 6 months, defrosting before baking.

Oaty Cherry Cookies

9oz butter, softened
2oz caster sugar
3½oz light muscovado sugar
5½oz self-raising flour
8oz porridge oats
7oz glacé cherries
2oz raisins

Takes 30 minutes • Makes 18

1 Preheat oven to 350°F. Line 2 or 3 baking sheets with non-stick baking paper (or bake in batches). In a bowl, beat the butter and sugars together until light and fluffy. Stir in the flour and oats and mix well. Roughly chop three quarters of the cherries, then stir these and the whole cherries and raisins into the oat mixture.

2 Divide the mixture into 18 equal portions. Roughly shape each portion into a ball. Put on the baking sheets well apart to allow for spreading. Lightly flatten each biscuit with your fingertips, keeping the mixture quite rough-looking.

3 Bake for 15–20 minutes until the cookies are pale golden around the edges, but still feel soft in the center. Cool on the baking sheets for 5 minutes, then transfer to a wire rack.

• Per cookie 249 calories, protein 2g, carbohydrate 33g, fat 13g, saturated fat 7g, fiber 1g, added sugar 15g, salt 0.36g

Swap the sultanas for chopped nuts or other dried fruit to vary the recipe for these cookies.

Lemon and Sultana Cookies

12oz plain flour
½ tsp baking powder
½ tsp baking soda
5oz butter, cut into small pieces
6oz caster sugar
3oz white raisins
4oz lemon curd
2 eggs, beaten

FOR THE ICING
4oz sifted icing sugar
2 tbsp fresh lemon juice

Takes 30 minutes • Makes 30

1 Preheat oven to 400°F. Butter 3 baking sheets (or bake in several batches). Sift the flour, baking powder and bicarbonate of soda into a bowl. Add the butter and rub in with your fingertips until the mixture resembles fine breadcrumbs.

2 Stir in the sugar and sultanas, add the lemon curd and eggs and mix to a soft dough. Shape the dough into 30 small balls, about 1in wide, and put on the baking sheets, allowing plenty of space between them so they can spread. Using your fingers, gently press the top of each biscuit to flatten it slightly.

3 Bake for 12–15 minutes until risen and light golden. Leave to cool for 1 minute on the baking sheets, then transfer to a wire rack to cool completely. Blend the icing sugar and lemon juice, then drizzle over each cookie.

• Per cookie 134 calories, protein 2g, carbohydrate 23g, fat 5g, saturated fat 3g, fiber trace, added sugar 11g, salt 0.2g

Traditionally made with vegetable shortening, this old-fashioned type of cookie dough can also be made into a shell for a fruit tart.

Pine Nut Cookies

2oz pine nuts, plus a few extra
6oz butter, softened
5oz golden granulated sugar,
plus extra for sprinkling
seeds from 1 star anise, crushed
(optional)
1 egg
9oz plain flour
1 tsp baking powder

Takes 1 hour • Makes 18

1 Toast the pine nuts in a dry, heavy-based pan for 1–2 minutes. Set aside.
2 Put the butter, sugar and star anise seeds, if using, in a food processor and whiz for 1 minute. Scrape down the bowl, then whiz again briefly. Add the egg and whiz again. Tip in the flour and baking powder and whiz until the mixture forms a dough. Mix in the pine nuts (reserving enough for step 3), then chill for 30 minutes, wrapped in plastic film.
3 Preheat oven to 350°F. Take walnut-sized pieces of dough and press out into 2in rounds, level but not too neat. Put on the baking sheets and press two pine nuts on the top of each. Bake for 15 minutes until pale golden. Transfer to a wire rack to cool, sprinkle with sugar and serve.

• Per cookie 176 calories, protein 2g, carbohydrate 20g, fat 10g, saturated fat 5g, fiber trace, added sugar 9g, salt 0.28g

Serve with ripe Taleggio or another soft cheese, such as dolcelatte or St. Andre, and a brimming bowl of fresh, juicy strawberries.

Walnut Oat Biscuits

4oz butter, softened
3oz light muscovado sugar
1 egg, beaten
2oz porridge oats
2oz walnuts, finely chopped
3oz plain flour
½ tsp baking powder
cheese and strawberries, to serve

Takes 25 minutes • Makes 15

1 Preheat oven to 350ºF. Butter two baking sheets. In a bowl, beat the butter and sugar for 5 minutes by hand or 2 minutes in the food processor until light and fluffy. Beat in the egg, then stir in the oats, nuts, flour and baking powder.

2 Drop dessertspoonfuls of the mixture, with a little space between, on the baking sheets. Bake for 15 minutes until pale golden, then cool on a wire rack.

3 Serve as described above with the cheese and strawberries. The biscuits will keep fresh in a sealed container for up to a week.

• Per biscuit 133 calories, protein 2g, carbohydrate 13g, fat 9g, saturated fat 4g, fiber 1g, added sugar 6g, salt 0.15g

Eat these mouth-watering cookies while they're still warm – that way the chocolate is still gorgeously gooey in the middle.

Chunky Choc Orange Cookies

9oz butter, softened
2oz caster sugar
3½oz light muscovado sugar
10oz self-raising flour
2 tbsp milk
6oz orange-flavored dark chocolate, very roughly chopped
2oz pecan nuts, very roughly chopped

Takes 30 minutes • Makes 18

1 Preheat oven to 350°F. Line 2 or 3 baking sheets with non-stick baking paper (or bake in batches). In a bowl, beat together the butter and sugars until light and fluffy. Stir in the flour and milk, mix well, then stir in the chocolate and nuts.

2 Divide the mixture into 18 equal portions. Roughly shape each portion into a ball. Put on the baking sheets well apart to allow for spreading. Lightly flatten each biscuit with your fingertips, keeping the mixture quite rough-looking.

3 Bake for 15–20 minutes until the cookies are pale golden around the edges, but still feel soft in the center. Cool on the baking sheets for 5 minutes, then transfer to a wire rack and allow to cool a little more before eating.

• Per cookie 261 calories, protein 2g, carbohydrate 28g, fat 16g, saturated fat 9g, fiber 1g, added sugar 14g, salt 0.42g

Light biscuits with a surprise almond filling
and orange-scented sugar.

Festive Almond Biscuits

3oz unsalted butter, chilled and
cut into pieces
4oz self-raising flour
3oz ground almonds
4oz caster sugar
2oz marzipan, cut into 20 cubes

FOR THE ORANGE SUGAR
pared rind of 2 oranges
2oz icing sugar

Takes 1¼ hours • Makes 20

1 Whiz the butter with the flour and almonds
to a breadcrumb consistency. Add half the
caster sugar; whiz until the mixture starts to
cling together, then work lightly into a ball.
2 Thinly roll out half of the dough. Use 2½in
cutters to cut out crescents and stars; put 20
on a buttered baking sheet. Roll the marzipan
cubes into sausage- or ball- shaped pieces
and lay on the crecents and stars. Top each
with matching dough shape and seal the
edges. Chill for 30 minutes.
3 Preheat the oven to 325ºF. Put the orange
rind on a baking sheet and bake for 3
minutes; cool. Mix the remaining caster sugar
and the icing sugar; toss with the rind. Bake
the biscuits for 18–20 minutes; cool on a
wire rack. Sprinkle with the orange sugar.

• Per biscuit 109 calories, protein 1g, carbohydrate
14g, fat 6g, saturated fat 2g, fiber 1g, added sugar 9g,
salt 0.06g

These delicious biscuits were made to send to the ANZACs (Australian and New Zealand Army Corps) serving in Gallipoli.

Anzac Biscuits

3oz porridge oats
3oz desiccated coconut
4oz plain flour
4oz caster sugar
4oz butter, melted
1 tbsp golden syrup
1 tsp baking of soda

Takes 35 minutes • Makes 20

1 Preheat oven to 350ºF. Put the oats, coconut, flour and sugar in a bowl. Melt the butter in a small pan or microwave and stir in the golden syrup. Add the bicarbonate of soda to 2 tablespoons boiling water, then stir into the golden syrup and butter mixture.

2 Make a well in the middle of the dry ingredients and pour in the butter and golden syrup mixture. Stir gently to incorporate the dry ingredients.

3 Put dessertspoonfuls of the mixture on to buttered baking sheets, about 1in apart to allow room for spreading. Bake in batches for 8–10 minutes until golden. Transfer to a wire rack to cool.

• Per biscuit 118 calories, protein 1g, carbohydrate 13g, fat 7g, saturated fat 5g, fiber 1g, added sugar 6g, salt 0.28g

Index

Picture credits and recipe credits

BBC Worldwide would like to thank the following for providing photographs. While every effort has been made to trace and acknowledge all photographers, we would like to apologize should there be any errors or omissions.

Marie-Louise Avery p30, p44, p82, p142, p144, p146, p156, p194; Steve Baxter p138; Martin Brigdale p14, p64, p118; Linda Burgess p24, p38, p46, p66, p72, p100, p108, p140; Jean Cazals p200; Gus Filgate p210; Anna Hodgson p136; David Munns p10, p56, p60, p68, p114, p170, p176; Myles New p18; Michael Paul p26, p28, p84, p98, p104, p132, p162, p166, p192;

Craig Robertson p6, p36, p50; Howard Shooter p12; Simon Smith p102, p208; Simon Smith/Adrian Taylor p168; Roger Stowell p42, p52, p54, p62, p74, p92, p116, p124, p160, p188, p202, p204; Adrian Taylor/Bill Reavell/ Niall McDiarmid p22; Martin Thompson p128; Ian Wallace p16; Philip Webb p32, p34, p40, p58, p76, p80, p88, p106, p112, p152, p164, p172, p178, p184, p186, p190; Simon Wheeler p20, p78, p86, p110, p122, p130, p134, p150, p154, p158, p182, p198, p206; Jonathan Whittaker p148; Geoff Wilkinson p48, p90, p94, p126, p174; Tim Young p70, p96, p120, p180, p196.

Thanks also to the contributors to *BBC Good Food Magazine* and the editorial team, who created the recipes in this book.

Barbara Baker, Sara Buenfeld, Mary Cadogan, Jane Clarke, Linda Collister, Alison Cork, Roz Denny, Matthew Drennan, Lewis Esson, Joanna Farrow, Margaret Fineran, Silvana Franco, Moyra Fraser, Brian Glover, Carole Handslip, Alastair Hendy, Margaret Hickey, Carrie Hill, Geraldene Holt, Fiona Hunter, Sue Lawrence, Orlando Murrin, Vicky Musselman, Jane Newdick, Angela Nilson, Thane Prince, Rosie Squire, Sue Style, Jenny White, Mitzie Wilson, Antony Worrall Thompson and Jeni Wright.